interchange

THIRD EDITION

Jack C. Richards
with *Jonathan Hull* and *Susan Proctor*

STUDENT'S BOOK

PUBLISHED BY THE PRESS SYNDICATE OF THE UNIVERSITY OF CAMBRIDGE
The Pitt Building, Trumpington Street, Cambridge, United Kingdom

CAMBRIDGE UNIVERSITY PRESS
The Edinburgh Building, Cambridge CB2 2RU, UK
40 West 20th Street, New York, NY 10011–4211, USA
477 Williamstown Road, Port Melbourne, VIC 3207, Australia
Ruiz de Alarcón 13, 28014 Madrid, Spain
Nautica Building, The Water Club, Beach Road, Granger Bay, Cape Town 8005, South Africa

http://www.cambridge.org

© Cambridge University Press 2005

First published 2005
Interchange Third Edition Student's Book 3 has been developed from *New Interchange* Student's Book 3,
first published by Cambridge University Press in 1998.
Printed in Hong Kong, China
Typeface New Century Schoolbook   *System* QuarkXPress®

ISBN 0 521 60218 1 Student's Book 3
ISBN 0 521 60216 5 Student's Book 3 w/Self-study Audio CD
ISBN 0 521 60217 3 Student's Book 3 w/Self-study Audio CD
                         (Korea edition)
ISBN 0 521 60220 3 Student's Book 3A w/Self-study Audio CD
ISBN 0 521 60221 1 Student's Book 3B w/Self-study Audio CD
ISBN 0 521 60222 X Workbook 3
ISBN 0 521 60223 8 Workbook 3A
ISBN 0 521 60224 6 Workbook 3B
ISBN 0 521 60225 4 Teacher's Edition 3
ISBN 0 521 60229 7 Class Audio Cassettes 3
ISBN 0 521 60227 0 Self-study Audio Cassette 3
ISBN 0 521 60228 9 Class Audio CDs 3
ISBN 0 521 60230 0 Self-study Audio CD 3
ISBN 0 521 60232 7 Lab Guide 3
ISBN 0 521 61342 6 Lab Audio CDs 3
ISBN 0 521 95055 4 Class Audio Cassette Sampler
ISBN 0 521 95056 2 Class Audio CD Sampler
ISBN 0 521 95053 8 Classroom Language Posters

Also available
ISBN 0 521 61346 9 Video 3 (DVD)
ISBN 0 521 60233 5 Video 3 (NTSC)
ISBN 0 521 60234 3 Video 3 (PAL)
ISBN 0 521 60236 X Video Activity Book 3
ISBN 0 521 60237 8 Video Teacher's Guide 3
ISBN 0 521 91481 7 Video Sampler (NTSC)
ISBN 0 521 60238 6 Interchange Third Edition/Passages
                         Placement and Evaluation Package

Forthcoming
ISBN 0 521 60226 2 Teacher's Resource Book 3
ISBN 0 521 60239 4 Interchange Third Edition/Passages
                         Placement and Evaluation CD-ROM

Art direction, book design, photo research, and layout services: Adventure House, NYC
Audio production: Richard LePage & Associates

Richards, Jack Croft
ریچاردز، جک کرافت، ۱۹۴۳- م
(اینترچنج ۳: استیودنت بوک)
Interchang 3: student book (Third edition) / Jack C.Richards
تهران: جنگل، ۱۳۸۵=۲۰۰۶م.
۱۵۲،۷ص.: مصور (رنگی).
انگلیسی.
فهرست نویسی بر اساس اطلاعات فیپا.
افست ازروی چاپ ۲۰۰۵ دانشگاه کمبریج.
۱. زبان انگلیسی -- کتابهای درسی برای خارجیان. ۲. ارتباط بین المللی
-- مسائل، تمرینها و غیره. الف. عنوان: Interchang 3: student book
(Third edition).
۴۲۸/۲۴   PE ۱۱۲۸/ر۸۳م۹۶ر۷۲
۱۳۸۵
کتابخانه ملی ایران
۸۵–۱۴۴۲م

شناسنامه کتاب
نام کتاب: interchange 3 (third edition):
Student book
نویسنده: Jack C.Richards
تاریخ و نوبت چاپ: هفتم
تیراژ: ۱۰۰۰۰ جلد
مجتمع لیتوگرافی، چاپ و صحافی جنگل
ناشر: انتشارات جنگل (Jungle Publications)
تلفن:
021-66495275-66486115-9
0311-2212047-2239809

www.junglepub.org

To the student

Welcome to *Interchange Third Edition*! This revised edition of *New Interchange* gives you many more opportunities to learn and practice English. We are confident this book will help you improve your English! The course combines topics, functions, and grammar. You will learn the four skills of listening, speaking, reading, and writing, in addition to vocabulary and pronunciation.

Each book has 16 units divided into sections, and each section has its own purpose. The **Snapshot** usually introduces the unit's topic with real-world information. The **Word Power** presents new vocabulary. **Perspectives** is a new section that uses people's opinions and experiences about a topic to present new grammar. The **Conversation** is a natural, fun dialog that introduces new grammar. You then see and practice this language in the **Grammar Focus**. The **Pronunciation** exercises help you sound like a native speaker.

In the **Listening** section you hear people speaking in many different contexts. You talk in pairs, in groups, or as a class with the many **Speaking** activities. In the **Interchange activities** you talk even more freely about yourself. These fun activities let you share your own ideas and opinions. In the **Writing** section you write about yourself and your classmates. Finally, at the end of each unit, you read about and further discuss the unit's topic in the **Reading** section.

Frequent **Progress checks** let you check your own development. In these self-assessment exercises *you* decide what material you need to review.

The **Self-study Audio CD** contains the conversations from the unit for extra listening practice. Your CD also has a section with new, original audio material. You can use this in class, in a lab, or at home with the Self-study exercises at the back of this book.

We think you'll enjoy using this book and hope you become better, more confident learners of English. Good luck!

Jack C. Richards
Jonathan Hull
Susan Proctor

Authors' acknowledgments

A great number of people contributed to the development of *Interchange Third Edition*. Particular thanks are owed to the following:

The **reviewers** using *New Interchange* in the following schools and institutes – their insights and suggestions have helped define the content and format of the third edition: Gino Pumadera, **American School**, Guayaquil, Ecuador; Don Ahn, **APEX**, Seoul, Korea; teachers at **AUA Language Center**, Bangkok, Thailand; Linda Martinez, **Canada College**, Redwood City, California, USA; Rosa Maria Valencia Rodriguez, **CEMARC**, Mexico City, Mexico; Wendel Mendes Dantas, **Central Universitária**, São Paulo, Brazil; Lee Altschuler, **Cheng Kung University**, Tainan, Taiwan; Chun Mao Le, **Cheng Siu Institute of Technology**, Kaohsiung, Taiwan; Selma Alfonso, **Colégio Arquidiocesano**, São Paulo, Brazil; Daniel de Mello Ferraz, **Colégio Camargo Aranha**, São Paulo, Brazil; Paula dos Santos Dames, **Colegio Militar do Rio de Janeiro**, Rio de Janeiro, Brazil; Elizabeth Ortiz, **COPOL-COPEI**, Guayaquil, Ecuador; Alexandre de Oliveira, **First Idiomas**, São Paulo, Brazil; João Franco Júnior, **2B Idiomas**, São Paulo, Brazil; Jo Ellen Kaiser and David Martin, **Fort Lauderdale High School**, Fort Lauderdale, Florida, USA; Azusa Okada, **Hiroshima Shudo University**, Hiroshima, Japan; Sandra Herrera and Rosario Valdiria, **INACAP**, Santiago, Chile; Samara Camilo Tome Costa, **Instituto Brasil-Estados Unidos**, Rio de Janeiro, Brazil; Eric Hamilton, **Instituto Chileno Norteamericano de Cultura**, Santiago, Chile; **ICNA**, Santiago, Chile; Pedro Benites, Carolina Chenett, Elena Montero Hurtado, Patricia Nieto, and Antonio Rios, **Instituto Cultural Peruano Norteamericano (ICPNA)**, Lima, Peru; Vanclei Nascimento, **Instituto Pentágono**, São Paulo, Brazil; Michael T. Thornton, **Interactive College of Technology**, Chamblee, Georgia, USA; Norma Aguilera Celis, **IPN ESCA Santo Tomas**, Mexico City, Mexico; Lewis Barksdale, **Kanazawa Institute of Technology**, Ishikawa, Japan; Clare St. Lawrence, Gill Christie, and Sandra Forrester, **Key Language Services**, Quito, Ecuador; Érik Mesquita, **King's Cross**, São Paulo, Brazil; Robert S. Dobie, **Kojen English Language Schools**, Taipei, Taiwan; Shoko Miyagi, **Madison Area Technical College**, Madison, Wisconsin, USA; Atsuko K. Yamazaki, **Institute of Technologists**, Saitama, Japan; teachers and students at **Institute of Technologists**, Saitama, Japan; Gregory Hadley, **Niigata University of International and Information Studies**, Niigata, Japan; Tony Brewer and Frank Claypool, **Osaka College of Foreign Languages and International Business**, Osaka, Japan; Chris Kerr, **Osaka University of Economics and Law**, Osaka, Japan; Angela Suzete Zumpano, **Personal Language Center**, São Paulo, Brazil; Simon Banha Jr. and Tomas S. Martins, **Phil Young's English School**, Curitiba, Brazil; Mehran Sabet and Bob Diem, **Seigakuin University**, Saitama, Japan; Lily Beam, **Shie Jen University**, Kaohsiung, Taiwan; Ray Sullivan, **Shibuya Kyoiku Gakuen Makuhari Senior and Junior High School**, Chiba, Japan; Robert Gee, **Sugiyama Jogakuen University**, Nagoya, Japan; Arthur Tu, **Taipei YMCA**, Taipei, Taiwan; Hiroko Nishikage, Alan Hawk, Peter Riley, and Peter Anyon, **Taisho University**, Tokyo, Japan; Vera Berk, **Talkative Idiomas**, São Paulo, Brazil; Patrick D. McCoy, **Toyo University**, Saitama, Japan; Kathleen Krokar and Ellen D. Sellergren, **Truman College**, Chicago, Illinois, USA; Gabriela Cortes Sanchez, **UAM-A**, Mexico City, Mexico; Marco A. Mora Piedra, **Universidad de Costa Rica**, San Jose, Costa Rica; Janette Carvalhinho de Oliveira, **Universidade Federal do Espirito Santo**, Vitoria, Brazil; Belem Saint Martin Lozada, **Universidad ISEC**, Colegio del Valle, Mexico City, Mexico; Robert Sanchez Flores, **Universidad Nacional Autonoma de Mexico**, Centro de Lenguas Campus Aragon, Mexico City, Mexico; Bertha Chela de Rodriguez, **Universidad Simòn Bolìvar**, Caracas, Venezuela; Marilyn Johnson, **Washoe High School**, Reno, Nevada, USA; Monika Soens, **Yen Ping Senior High School**, Taipei, Taiwan; Kim Yoon Gyong, **Yonsei University**, Seoul, Korea; and Tania Borges Lobao, **York Language Institute**, Rio de Janeiro, Brazil.

The **editorial** and **production** team:
David Bohlke, Jeff Chen, Yuri Hara, Pam Harris, Paul Heacock, Louisa Hellegers, Lise R. Minovitz, Pat Nelson, Bill Paulk, Danielle Power, Mary Sandre, Tami Savir, Kayo Taguchi, Louisa van Houten, Mary Vaughn, Jennifer Wilkin, and Dorothy Zemach.

And Cambridge University Press **staff** and **advisors**:
Jim Anderson, Angela Andrade, Mary Louise Baez, Carlos Barbisan, Kathleen Corley, Kate Cory-Wright, Elizabeth Fuzikava, Steve Golden, Cecilia Gomez, Heather Gray, Bob Hands, Pauline Ireland, Ken Kingery, Gareth Knight, Nigel McQuitty, João Madureira, Andy Martin, Alejandro Martinez, Carine Mitchell, Mark O'Neil, Tom Price, Dan Schulte, Catherine Shih, Howard Siegelman, Ivan Sorrentino, Alcione Tavares, Koen Van Landeghem, and Ellen Zlotnick.

Plan of Book 3

Titles/Topics	Speaking	Grammar
UNIT 1 PAGES 2-7		
That's what friends are for! Personality types and qualities; relationships; turn ons and turn offs	Describing personalities; expressing likes and dislikes; agreeing and disagreeing; complaining	Relative pronouns as subjects and objects; clauses with *it* + adverbial clauses with *when*
UNIT 2 PAGES 8-13		
Career moves Jobs; unusual careers; job skills; summer jobs	Talking about unusual careers; describing jobs; discussing the pros and cons of jobs	Gerund phrases as subjects and objects; comparisons with adjectives, verbs, nouns, and past participles
PROGRESS CHECK PAGES 14-15		
UNIT 3 PAGES 16-21		
Could you do me a favor? Favors; formal and informal requests; messages	Making unusual requests; making indirect requests; accepting and declining requests	Requests with modals, *if* clauses, and gerunds; indirect requests
UNIT 4 PAGES 22-27		
What a story! The media; news stories; exceptional events	Narrating a story; describing events in the past	Past continuous vs. simple past; past perfect
PROGRESS CHECK PAGES 28-29		
UNIT 5 PAGES 30-35		
Crossing cultures Cultural comparisons and culture shock; moving abroad; emotions; customs; tourism and travel abroad	Talking about moving abroad; expressing emotions; describing cultural expectations; giving advice	Noun phrases containing relative clauses; expectations: *the custom to, (not) supposed to, expected to, (not) acceptable to*
UNIT 6 PAGES 36-41		
What's wrong with it? Consumer complaints; everyday problems; electronics; repairs	Describing problems; making complaints; explaining something that needs to be done	Describing problems with past participles as adjectives and with nouns; describing problems with *keep* + gerund, *need* + gerund, and *need* + passive infinitive
PROGRESS CHECK PAGES 42-43		
UNIT 7 PAGES 44-49		
The world we live in The environment; world problems; current issues	Identifying and describing problems; coming up with solutions	Passive in the present continuous and present perfect; prepositions of cause; infinitive clauses and phrases
UNIT 8 PAGES 50-55		
Lifelong learning Education; learner choices; strategies for learning; personal qualities	Asking about preferences; discussing pros and cons of different college majors; talking about learning methods; talking about personal qualities	*Would rather* and *would prefer*; *by* + gerund to describe how to do things
PROGRESS CHECK PAGES 56-57		

Pronunciation/Listening	Writing/Reading	Interchange Activity
Linked sounds Listening for opinions; listening for descriptions of people *Self-study*: Listening for likes and dislikes about people	Writing a description of a best friend "You Have to Have Friends": Reading about making and keeping friends	"Personality types": Interviewing a classmate to find out about personality characteristics
Stress with compound nouns Listening to descriptions of summer jobs; listening for likes and dislikes *Self-study*: Listening to descriptions of careers; listening for comparisons	Writing about career advantages and disadvantages "Strategies for Keeping Your Job": Reading advice about behavior in the workplace	"The dinner party": Comparing people's careers and personalities to make a seating chart for a dinner party
Unreleased consonants Listening to people making, accepting, and declining requests *Self-study*: Listening to people making plans, asking for a favor, and giving an excuse	Writing an informal e-mail request "Yes or No?": Reading about the way people in different cultures respond "yes" and "no"	"Borrowers and lenders": Asking classmates to borrow items; lending or refusing to lend items
Intonation in complex sentences Listening to news broadcasts; listening to a narrative about a past event *Self-study*: Listening to a news story	Writing a newspaper article "Strange but True": Reading tabloid articles about sensational events	"A double ending": Completing a story with two different endings
Word stress in sentences Listening for information about living abroad; listening to opinions about customs *Self-study*: Listening to people's concerns about traveling abroad	Writing a tourist pamphlet "Culture Shock": Reading journal entries about moving to another country	"Culture check": Comparing customs in different countries
Contrastive stress Listening to people exchange things in a store; listening to complaints; listening to repair people describe their jobs *Self-study*: Listening to people's problems with items they bought	Writing a letter of complaint "Trading Spaces": Reading about a TV show in which participants redecorate other people's rooms	"Fixer-upper": Comparing problems in two pictures of an apartment
Reduction of auxiliary verbs Listening to environmental problems; listening for solutions *Self-study*: Listening to people talk about problems in their city	Writing a letter to the editor "The Threat to Kiribati": Reading about an island that is sinking into the ocean	"Make your voices heard!": Choosing an issue and deciding on an effective method of protest; devising a strategy
Intonation in questions of choice Listening to descriptions of courses; listening for additional information *Self-study*: Listening to a student describe online classes	Writing a short speech "Learning Styles": Reading about different kinds of learning	"Learning curves": Choosing between different things you want to learn

Titles/Topics	Speaking	Grammar

Pronunciation/Listening	Writing/Reading	Interchange Activity
Sentence stress Listening to suggestions for self-improvement *Self-study*: Listening for what people need to have done	Writing a letter of advice "Improve Your Memory, Improve Your Life": Reading about techniques to improve memory	"Because I said so!": Discussing different points of view of parents and their children
Syllable stress Listening for opinions about public figures; listening to predictions *Self-study*: Listening to past events; making predictions	Writing a biography "The Global Village": Reading about political and technological changes that bring people closer together	"History buff": Taking a history quiz
Reduction of *have* and *been* Listening to descriptions of important events; listening to regrets and explanations *Self-study*: Listening to people describe changes in themselves	Writing a letter of apology "If You Could Do It All Again": Reading about people's life choices and regrets	"If things were different . . .": Imagining different possibilities for the way things have turned out
Reduced words Listening for features and slogans *Self-study*: Listening for qualities that help people make friends more easily	Writing a TV commercial "The Wrong Stuff": Reading about advertising failures	"Entrepreneurs": Designing a business plan for a small business
Reduction in past modals Listening to explanations; listening for the best solution *Self-study*: Listening to situations and reacting	Writing about a predicament "The Blue Lights of Silver Cliff": Reading a story about an unexplained phenomenon	"Photo plays": Drawing possible conclusions about situations
Stress in compound nouns Listening to a producer describe his work; listening for personality traits *Self-study*: Listening to an interview; listening for steps in a process	Writing about a process "Hooray for Bollywood!": Reading about the kind of movies made in India	"Who makes it happen?": Putting together a crew for making a movie
Intonation in tag questions Listening for solutions to everyday annoyances; listening to issues and opinions *Self-study*: Listening to concerns about issues and problems	Writing a letter to a community leader "How Serious Is Plagiarism?": Reading about plagiarism and people's opinions about its severity	"You be the judge!": Setting rules for common offenses
Stress and rhythm Listening to challenges and rewards of people's work; listening for people's goals for the future *Self-study*: Listening to a person's experience in the Peace Corps	Writing a personal statement for an application "Young and Gifted": Reading about exceptionally gifted young people	"Viewpoints": Taking a survey about volunteering

1 That's what friends are for!

1 SNAPSHOT

Love and Marriage
in North America

What women look for in a partner	What men look for in a partner
• leadership qualities	• physical attractiveness
• earnings potential	• warmth and affection
• a sense of humor	• homemaking ability
• intelligence	• fashion sense
• job skills	• social skills
• success	• sensitivity

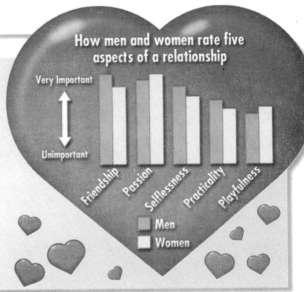

How men and women rate five aspects of a relationship

Very Important

Unimportant

Friendship Passion Selflessness Practicality Playfulness

☐ Men
☐ Women

Source: *Weekly World News*

In your opinion, which of the qualities above are most important to look for in a partner?
Are there other important qualities missing from the lists?
How do people meet their partners in your country?

2 CONVERSATION I like guys who . . .

A ▶ Listen and practice.

Chris: Do you have a date for the party yet?
Kim: Actually, I don't. . . . Do you know anyone I could go with?
Chris: Hmm. What kind of guys do you like?
Kim: Oh, I like guys who aren't too serious and who have a good sense of humor. You know, someone like you.
Chris: OK. Uh, what else?
Kim: Well, I'd prefer someone I have something in common with – who I can talk to easily.
Chris: I think I know just the guy for you. Bob Branson. Do you know him?
Kim: No, I don't think so.
Chris: OK, I'll ask him to meet us for coffee, and you can tell me what you think.

B ▶ Listen to Chris and Kim discuss Bob after they met for coffee. How did Kim like him?

3 GRAMMAR FOCUS

Relative pronouns ▷

Relative pronouns as subjects

I like **guys**. **They** aren't too serious. → I like guys **who/that** aren't too serious.

I like **guys**. **They** have a good sense of humor. → I like guys **who/that** have a good sense of humor.

Relative pronouns as objects

I'd prefer **someone**. I can talk to **him** easily. → I'd prefer someone (**who/that**) I can talk to easily.

I'd prefer **someone**. I have fun with **him**. → I'd prefer someone (**who/that**) I have fun with.

A *Pair work* Match the information in columns A and B. Then rewrite each pair to form one sentence. Use a relative pronoun if necessary.

A

1. I don't want to have a partner ...*d*...
2. I'd like to meet people ....
3. I'd prefer a roommate ....
4. I don't like to be with people ....
5. I want to discuss my problems with friends ....
6. I'd rather have a boss ....
7. I'd prefer to have teachers ....

B

a. These people are organized and intelligent.
b. This person has good leadership qualities.
c. These people have a good sense of humor.
d. I have nothing in common with this person.
e. These people are warm and sensitive.
f. I don't feel comfortable around these people.
g. This person is quiet and considerate.

> 1. I don't want to have a partner who I have nothing in common with.

B *Pair work* Complete the sentences in column A with your own information. Then compare with a partner. Do you and your partner have similar opinions?

4 WORD POWER Personalities

A Match the words with the definitions. Then decide which words are positive and which are negative. Write **P** or **N** next to each word.

...*f*... 1. sociable ..*P*..
.... 2. intolerant ....
.... 3. modest ....
.... 4. temperamental ....
.... 5. egotistical ....
.... 6. easygoing ....
.... 7. stingy ....
.... 8. unreliable ....
.... 9. supportive ....

a. a person who won't accept other people's differences
b. someone who doesn't like giving things to people; ungenerous
c. someone who expresses a very high opinion of him- or herself
d. someone who is helpful and encouraging
e. a person who doesn't do what he or she promised
f. a person who enjoys being with other people
g. a person who has unpredictable or irregular moods
h. a person who doesn't worry much or get angry easily
i. someone who doesn't brag about his or her accomplishments

B *Pair work* Can you remember the definitions? Take turns talking about the adjectives.

"A sociable person is someone who . . ."

C *Pair work* Think of at least three adjectives to describe yourself. Then tell a partner.

5 LISTENING What are they like?

A ▶ Listen to conversations that describe three people. Are the descriptions positive (**P**) or negative (**N**)? Check (✓) the box.

1. Andrea	☐ P	☐ N	....
2. James	☐ P	☐ N	....
3. Mr. Johnson	☐ P	☐ N	....

B ▶ Listen again. Write two adjectives for each person in the chart.

6 DISCUSSION Ideal people

A *Group work* What is the ideal parent, friend, or partner like? What is one quality each should have and one quality each should *not* have? Complete the chart.

	This person should be . . .	This person should not be . . .
The ideal parent	....	....
The ideal friend	....	....
The ideal partner	....	....

B *Group work* Take turns describing your "ideal people." Try to agree on the two most important qualities for a parent, a friend, and a partner.

A: I think the ideal parent is someone who is easygoing.
B: I agree. The ideal parent is someone who doesn't get upset easily and who isn't temperamental.
C: Oh, I'm not sure I agree. . . .

7 WRITING About a best friend

A *Pair work* Talk about your best friend. Then write a paragraph.

> *My best friend is someone who is sensitive about my feelings. She's a person who is very supportive and always listens to my problems. . . .*

B *Pair work* Exchange paragraphs and follow these steps:

1. First, read your partner's paragraph for content. Ask follow-up questions for further information. Make notes.
2. Next, give suggestions about how the paragraph could be improved.
3. Then rewrite your paragraph to include your partner's suggestions.
4. Finally, check your paragraph for spelling, punctuation, and grammar.

8 PERSPECTIVES Quiz

A ▶ Listen to some common complaints. Check (✓) the ones you agree with.

Do you get ANNOYED easily?

☐ I don't like it when a cell phone rings in the classroom.

☐ It bothers me when a teacher forgets my name.

☐ I hate it when people talk with their mouth full.

☐ It upsets me when a close friend forgets my birthday.

☐ I can't stand it when people talk loudly to each other during a movie.

☐ I don't like it when people call me early in the morning.

☐ I can't stand it when a child screams in a restaurant.

☐ It bothers me when my doctor arrives late for an appointment.

Score: If you checked . . .
1–2 complaints: Wow! You don't get annoyed very easily.
3–4 complaints: You're fairly easygoing.
5–6 complaints: Hmm, you could be intolerant about some things.
7–8 complaints: Relax, you get annoyed too easily!

B Calculate your score. Do you get annoyed easily? Tell the class what bothers you the most.

9 PRONUNCIATION Linked sounds

A ▶ Listen and practice. Final consonant sounds are often linked to the vowel sounds that follow them.

It upsets me when a person is unreliable.

I love it when a friend is supportive and kind.

B ▶ Mark the linked sounds in the sentences below. Listen and check. Then practice saying the sentences.

1. I can't stand it when someone is late for an appointment.

2. Does it bother you when a friend is unreliable?

3. I hate it when a cell phone goes off in a performance.

C Take turns saying the sentences in Exercise 8. Pay attention to linked sounds.

That's what friends are for! • 5

10 GRAMMAR FOCUS

Clauses with it + adverbial clauses with when ▶

I don't mind **it**	**when** people talk loudly during a movie.
I don't like **it**	**when** a cell phone rings in the classroom.
I can't stand **it**	**when** a child screams in a restaurant.
It bothers me	**when** a teacher forgets my name.
It upsets me	**when** people arrive late for appointments.

A How do you feel about these situations? Complete the sentences with *it* clauses from the list. Then take turns reading your sentences with a partner.

I love it	It bothers me	I don't like it
I can't stand it	It embarrasses me	It doesn't bother me
It makes me happy	It really upsets me	I don't mind it

1. .... when someone gives me a compliment on my clothes.
2. .... when people are direct and say what's on their mind.
3. .... when someone corrects my English in front of others.
4. .... when a friend is sensitive and supportive.
5. .... when people throw trash on the ground.
6. .... when a friend treats me to dinner.
7. .... when I get phone calls on my birthday.
8. .... when a stranger asks me for money.
9. .... when people call me late at night.
10. .... when teachers are temperamental.

B *Group work* Do you ever get annoyed by a certain type of person or situation? Write down five things that annoy you the most. Then compare in groups.

A: I really can't stand it when people are stingy.
B: I feel the same way – especially when you've been generous to them!
C: Yeah, but it bothers me more when . . .

11 INTERCHANGE 1 Personality types

Interview a classmate to find out about his or her personality.
Go to Interchange 1 at the back of the book.

You Have to Have Friends

How do you choose your friends? What qualities do you look for in a friend?

People use the word "friend" in a variety of ways. A friend can mean anything from a casual acquaintance to someone you've known your whole life. Whoever they are, friends are an important part of life at every stage. They provide companionship and emotional support. Of all our relationships, friendships are the most voluntary. We choose our friends.

Making new friends
It's easy to stay in a circle of friends you're comfortable with. But as you get older, friendships may be lost – people move away or you just lose track of them. Building friendships is a lifelong, but worthwhile, job. New friendships can bring opportunities to experience new things.

A few pointers for making new friends:
• Reach out to others. Try to be open to new experiences and relationships.
• Participate in classes, clubs, or volunteer organizations. These activities will bring you into contact with people who share similar interests.
• Stick with it – even if you feel uncomfortable. It takes time to build friendships.

Keeping friends
Whether friendships are old or new, you can't neglect them if you want them to last. Even though it's sometimes hard to spend time together, it's important to keep in touch. Two other keys are flexibility and respect. Be understanding when plans change. If you find yourselves fighting, try to look at things from the other person's point of view.

Some tips for keeping friends:
• Be a good listener. Don't be judgmental and don't offer advice unless you're asked.
• Respect the other person's opinion, even when you don't agree.
• Never break a confidence. Your friends need to know they can trust you.
• Be supportive of your friends. It's important to love them despite their faults!

A Read the article. Then for each statement, check (✓) True, False, or Not given.

	True	False	Not given
1. You have to know someone a long time to be a friend.	☐	☐	☐
2. Friends are more important than family.	☐	☐	☐
3. New friendships allow you to learn new things.	☐	☐	☐
4. When you make new friends, old friends will be jealous.	☐	☐	☐
5. It's important to give your friends respect and support.	☐	☐	☐
6. You should always offer advice to your friends.	☐	☐	☐

B Find the phrases in *italics* in the text. Then choose the meaning for each phrase.

1. When you *lose track of* someone, you **can't locate** / **can't follow** him or her.
2. When you *reach out to* people, you try to **physically touch** / **connect with** them.
3. If you *stick with* something, you **give up on** / **continue to do** it.
4. When you *keep in touch*, you **communicate with** / **stay near to** someone.
5. If you *break a confidence*, you **tell a secret** / **depend on** someone.

C *Pair work* What other ways can you think of to make new friends? to keep friends?

Career moves

SNAPSHOT

Best Jobs Based on Personality Types

Artistic types like working with designs and patterns.

Clothing designer
Architect

Investigative types like figuring out problems.

Veterinarian
Pharmacist

Conventional types like following instructions and routines.

Air traffic controller
Accountant

Realistic types like working outside or with real-world materials.

Restaurant cook
Bus driver

Enterprising types like leading people and making decisions.

Flight attendant
Lawyer

Social types like working with other people.

High school coach
Child-care worker

Source: *Best Jobs for the 21st Century*

Can you think of two other jobs for each category? Compare your ideas with the class.
What personality type do you think you are?
Would you want to do the jobs listed under your personality type?

2 **PERSPECTIVES** *Career debate*

A ▶ Listen to the people talk about jobs. Do you agree or disagree?
Check (✓) the speaker you agree with more.

"Designing clothes is not a man's job. Women are much more fascinated by fashion."

"Not so! Many great clothing designers are men. Just look at Calvin Klein!"

"I would love to fly all the time. Being a flight attendant sounds exciting."

"I don't think so. Flight attendants get tired of traveling. They have to be away from their families all the time."

"I'd like to work for a newspaper, but writing a gossip column seems like an awful job."

"I don't agree! Finding out about famous people's lives could be really fun."

"I'd enjoy working with animals. I think being a veterinarian would be rewarding."

"I'm not so sure. Animals can be very unpredictable. Getting bitten by a dog would be scary!"

B Compare your responses with your classmates.

③ GRAMMAR FOCUS

Gerund phrases ▷

Gerund phrases as subjects

Designing clothes is not a man's job.
Being a flight attendant sounds exciting.
Writing a gossip column could be fun.
Directing a TV show would be interesting.

Gerund phrases as objects

He wouldn't like **being a fashion designer**.
He'd enjoy **being a flight attendant**.
She'd be good at **writing a gossip column**.
They'd love **directing a TV show**.

A Look at the gerund phrases in column A. Write your opinion of each job by choosing information from columns B and C. Then add two more gerund phrases and write similar sentences.

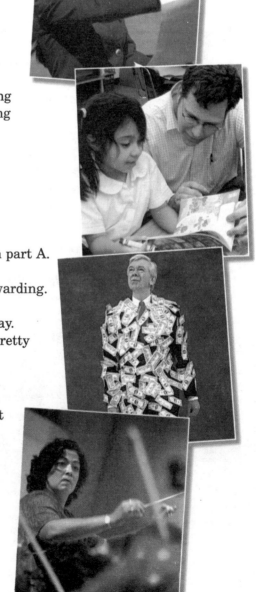

A	B	C
1. working as an architect	is	awful
2. taking care of children	seems	scary
3. winning the lottery	sounds	fantastic
4. conducting an orchestra	must be	fascinating
5. working on a movie set	could be	pretty difficult
6. making a living as an artist	would be	kind of boring
7. writing for a newspaper		really rewarding
8. retiring at age 40		very challenging
9.		
10.		

> *1. Working as an architect would be really rewarding.*

B *Pair work* Give reasons for your opinions about the jobs in part A.

A: In my opinion, working as an architect would be really rewarding.
B: Really? Why is that?
A: Because you could see people using your buildings every day.
B: I'm not so sure. For me, working as an architect must be pretty difficult, because . . .

C *Group work* Complete the sentences with gerund phrases. Then take turns reading your sentences. Share the three most interesting sentences with the class.

1. I think I'd be good at . . .
2. I wouldn't be very good at . . .
3. I'd be interested in . . .
4. I'd get tired of . . .
5. I'm very excited by . . .
6. I'd enjoy . . .

"I think I'd be good at figuring out problems."

4 WORD POWER Suffixes

A Add the suffixes *-er*, *-or*, *-ist*, or *-ian* to form the names of these jobs.
Write the words in the chart and add one more example to each column.

aerobics instruct ..*or*...   counsel ....   politic ....   TV report ....
comed ....   gossip column ....   psychiatr ....   Web design ....

-er	-or	-ist	-ian
	aerobics instructor		

B *Pair work* Can you give a definition for each job?

"An aerobics instructor is someone who teaches people how to do aerobic exercise."

5 SPEAKING Unusual careers

Group work Talk about an unusual career you would
like to have. Use information from Exercises 1–4 and your
own ideas. Other students ask follow-up questions.

A: I'd enjoy doing TV interviews with famous people.
B: Why is that?
A: Asking people about their lives would be fascinating.
C: Who would you interview?
A: Well, I think I'd be good at talking to politicians.

**"I'd be interested in interviewing
Arnold Schwarzenegger."**

6 WRITING Describing pros and cons

A Choose a job and make a list of its advantages. Then use the list to
write a paragraph about the job. Add a title.

> <u>Being a comedian: It's fun to be funny</u>
> Working as a comedian seems exciting. First of all,
> making people laugh would be a lot of fun, because you'd
> be laughing all the time, too. In addition, . . .

useful expressions
First of all, . . .
In addition, . . .
Further, . . .
On the other hand, . . .
For example, . . .

B *Pair work* Read your partner's paragraph. Then write a paragraph
about the disadvantages of your partner's job. Add a title.

C *Pair work* Read your partner's paragraph about your job's
disadvantages. Do you agree or disagree?

7 CONVERSATION *You get a great tan!*

A ▶ Listen and practice.

Tracy: Guess what . . . I've found a summer job!
Mark: That's great! Anything interesting?
Tracy: Yes, working at an amusement park.
Mark: Wow, that sounds fantastic!
Tracy: So, have *you* found anything?
Mark: Nothing yet, but I have a couple of leads.
   One is working as an intern for a record
   company – mostly answering phones.
   Or I can get a landscaping job again.
Tracy: Being an intern sounds more interesting
   than landscaping. You'd have better hours,
   and it's probably not as much work.
Mark: Yeah, but a landscaper earns more than
   an intern. And you get a great tan!

B ▶ Listen to the rest of the conversation.
What is Tracy going to do at the amusement park?

8 GRAMMAR FOCUS

Comparisons ▶

with adjectives	with verbs
. . . is **more interesting than** . . .	. . . earns **more than** . . .
. . . is **less interesting than** . . .	. . . earns **less than** . . .
. . . is **harder than** . . .	. . . earns **as much as** . . .
. . . is **not as hard as** . . .	. . . doesn't earn **as much as** . . .

with nouns	with past participles
. . . has **better/worse hours than** . . .	. . . is **better paid than** . . .
. . . isn't **as much work as** . . .	. . . isn't **as well paid as** . . .
. . . has **more education than** . . .	. . . is **better educated than** . . .

A Complete the sentences using the words in parentheses. Compare
with a partner. (More than one answer is possible.)

1. An interior decorator .... a fashion designer.   (paid)
2. A secret agent .... a police officer.   (travel)
3. An air traffic controller's job .... a TV director's job.   (artistic)
4. Landscapers .... veterinarians.   (education)
5. Working as a comedian .... being a public speaker.   (hard)
6. Aerobics instructors .... soccer coaches.   (earn)

B *Group work* Think of one more comparison for each pair of jobs in part A.

"An interior decorator doesn't work as late as a fashion designer."

9 PRONUNCIATION Stress with compound nouns

A ▶ Listen and practice. Notice that the first word in these compound nouns has more stress. Then add two more compound nouns to the chart.

⚪	⚪	⚪	⚪
bus driver	gossip columnist	choir director	....
taxi driver	newspaper reporter	orchestra conductor	....

B *Group work* Which job in each column would be more interesting? Why? Tell the group. Pay attention to stress.

10 LISTENING Summer jobs

A ▶ Listen to Carlos, Paul, and Julia talk about their summer jobs. Where does each person work? Write the name under each picture.

1. ....

2. ....

3. ....

B ▶ Listen again. Do they like their jobs? Why or why not?

11 ROLE PLAY Pros and cons

A *Group work* Each person chooses a job from the unit. Role-play a discussion using the job criteria in the box. Explain why your job is the worst!

A: I'm a teacher, and my salary is terrible!
B: I'm a doctor. I have a higher salary than a teacher, but a teacher has better hours.
C: Well, I'm a taxi driver. My hours aren't as bad as a doctor's, but . . .

B *Group work* Who has the worst job? Why? Tell the class.

job criteria

job security
level of difficulty
level of interest
salary
working conditions
working hours

12 INTERCHANGE 2 The dinner party

Would you be a good party planner? Go to Interchange 2 at the back of the book.

GRAMMAR FOCUS

Requests with modals, if clauses, and gerunds ▷

Less formal	**Can** I borrow your pencil?
	Could you lend me a jacket?
	Is it OK if I use your phone?
	Do you mind if I use your CD burner?
	Would it be OK if I picked it up on Friday night?
	Would you mind if I borrowed your digital camera?
	Would you mind letting me use your laptop?
	I wonder if I could borrow some money.
More formal	**I was wondering if you'd mind** lending me your car.

A Make requests using these cues. Then practice with a partner. Which requests need to be more formal?

1. You want to borrow your classmate's underwater camera for a diving trip.
   A: I was wondering . . .
   B: Sure, that's fine. But please be careful with it.

2. You want to use your roommate's computer.
   A: Is it OK . . . ?
   B: You can use it, but please save my work first.

3. Your neighbor has a car. You need a ride to class.
   A: . . .
   B: I'd be glad to. What time?

4. You want a friend to help you move on Saturday.
   A: . . .
   B: I'm really sorry. I'm busy the whole weekend.

5. You want to borrow your cousin's DVD of *Spider-Man*.
   A: . . .
   B: Actually, I already lent it to Serena. Sorry!

6. You would like a second piece of your aunt's cherry pie.
   A: . . .
   B: Yes, of course! Just pass me your plate.

B Rewrite these requests to make them more formal. Then practice making your requests with a partner. Accept or decline each request.

1. Lend me some money for an espresso.
2. Take these books back to the library for me.
3. Let me wear your leather jacket to the party this weekend.
4. I'd like to borrow your cell phone to call my friend in London.
5. Can I look at that newspaper when you've finished reading it?
6. Take care of my pet rabbit while I'm on vacation.

| Would you mind lending |
| me some money for |
| an espresso? |

4 PRONUNCIATION *Unreleased consonants*

A ▶ Listen and practice. Notice that when /t/, /d/, /k/, /g/, /p/, and /b/ are followed by other consonant sounds, they are unreleased.

Could Doug take care of my pet tarantula?

Can you ask Bob to sit behind Kate?

B ▶ Circle the unreleased consonants in the conversations. Listen and check. Then practice the conversations with a partner.

A: I wonder if I could borrow that book.
B: Yes, but can you take it back to Greg tomorrow?

A: Would you mind giving Albert some help moving that big bed?
B: Sorry, but my doctor said my back needs rest.

5 LISTENING *Favors*

A ▶ Listen to three telephone conversations. Write down what each caller requests. Does the other person agree to the request? Check (✓) Yes or No.

	Request	Yes	No
1. Tina	....	☐	☐
2. Mike	....	☐	☐
3. Phil	....	☐	☐

B *Pair work* Use the chart to act out each conversation.

6 WRITING *An informal e-mail request*

A Write an e-mail to a classmate asking for several favors. Explain why you need help.

B *Pair work* Exchange e-mails. Write a reply accepting or declining the requests.

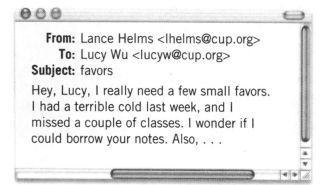

From: Lance Helms <lhelms@cup.org>
To: Lucy Wu <lucyw@cup.org>
Subject: favors
Hey, Lucy, I really need a few small favors.
I had a terrible cold last week, and I
missed a couple of classes. I wonder if I
could borrow your notes. Also, . . .

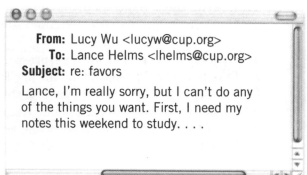

From: Lucy Wu <lucyw@cup.org>
To: Lance Helms <lhelms@cup.org>
Subject: re: favors
Lance, I'm really sorry, but I can't do any
of the things you want. First, I need my
notes this weekend to study. . . .

7 **INTERCHANGE 3** *Borrowers and lenders*

Find out how generous you are. Go to Interchange 3.

8 **WORD POWER** Collocations

A Which verb is *not* usually paired with each noun? Put
a line through the verb and compare with a partner.

1. (owe / offer / do / accept)   an apology
2. (do / return / make / receive)   a phone call
3. (return / do / ask for / make)   a favor
4. (receive / accept / turn down / offer)   an invitation
5. (make / deny / offer / refuse)   a request
6. (deny / receive / give / refuse)   a gift
7. (receive / return / do / give)   a compliment

B *Pair work* Choose five of the collocations in part A.
Then take turns using them to ask and answer questions.

A: When was the last time you owed someone an apology?
B: Well, just yesterday I spilled my soda all over you!

9 **PERSPECTIVES** *Could you tell Jeff . . . ?*

A Many people talked to Jeff's assistant while Jeff was away at
lunch today. Listen to their messages.

1. Could you tell Jeff that Tony is having a party on Friday night?

2. Can you ask Jeff to do me a favor and pick up a pizza on his way home?

3. Could you ask Jeff what he would like me to get him for his birthday?

4. Could you tell Jeff that there will be a staff meeting on Friday at 10:00?

5. Jeff is picking me up after basketball practice. Can you tell him not to be late?

6. Please tell Jeff that I owe him an apology – I forgot about our date last night.

7. Can you ask Jeff to return my call? I need to know when his report will be ready.

8. Could you ask Jeff whether he can come to class on Friday night instead of Thursday?

B Who do you think left each message? (More than one answer is possible.)

his boss   his girlfriend   his mother   his Spanish teacher   his younger sister

Could you do me a favor? • **19**

Indirect requests ▶

Statements	Indirect requests introduced by that
Jeff, Tony is having a party.	→ Could you tell Jeff **(that) Tony is having a party?**

Imperatives	Indirect requests using infinitives
Jeff, don't be late.	→ Can you tell Jeff **not to be late?**

Yes/No questions	Indirect requests introduced by if or whether
Sofia, are you free on Friday?	→ Can you ask Sofia **if she's free on Friday?**
Sofia, do you have my number?	→ Could you ask her **whether or not she has my number?**

Wh-questions	Indirect requests introduced by a question word
Jeff, when does the party start?	→ Can you ask Jeff **when the party starts?**
Sofia, what time should I pick you up?	→ Could you ask Sofia **what time I should pick her up?**

Rewrite these sentences as indirect requests. In other words, ask someone to deliver the message for you. Then compare with a partner.

1. Nina, can you do us a favor and drive us to the party?
2. Tony, how many friends can I bring to your party?
3. Sofia, are you going to the party with Jeff?
4. Kevin, did you accept the invitation to Tony's party?
5. Mario, are you going to give Tony a gift?
6. Anne-Marie, please return my phone call.
7. Dan, you owe me an apology for calling me after midnight!
8. Kimberly, I have to turn down your invitation to the movies.

> 1. Could you ask Nina if she can do us a favor and drive us to the party?

11 **SPEAKING** Pass it on.

A Write five unusual requests for your partner to pass on to classmates.

> Would you ask Jin Sook if she could lend me $100?

B *Class activity* Ask your partner to pass on your requests. Go around the class and make your partner's requests. Then tell your partner how people responded.

A: Would you ask Jin Sook if she could lend me $100?
B: Sure. . . . Jin Sook, could you lend Isam $100?
C: I'm sorry, but I can't! Could you tell Isam I'm broke?
B: Isam, Jin Sook says that she's broke.

YES or NO?

Scan the article. Where did the three events occur?

1 Living in a foreign culture can be exciting, but it can also be confusing. A group of Americans who taught English in other countries recently discussed their experiences. They decided that miscommunications were always possible, even over something as simple as "yes" and "no."

2 On her first day in Micronesia, Lisa thought people were ignoring her requests. The day was hot, and she needed a cold drink. She went into a store and asked, "Do you have cold drinks?" The woman there didn't say anything. Lisa rephrased the question. Still the woman said nothing. Lisa gave up and left the store. She later learned that the woman had answered her: She had raised her eyebrows, which in Micronesia means "yes."

3 This reminded Jan of an experience she had in Bulgaria. She had gone to a restaurant that was known for its stuffed cabbage. She asked the waiter, "Do you have stuffed cabbage today?" He nodded his head. Jan eagerly waited, but the cabbage never came. In that country, a nod means "no."

4 Tom had a similar problem when he arrived in India. After explaining something in class, he asked his students if they understood. They responded with many different nods and shakes of the head.

He assumed some people had not understood, so he explained again. When he asked again if they understood, they did the same thing. He soon found out that his students did understand. In India, people nod and shake their heads in different ways depending on where they come from. You have to know where a person is from to understand if they are indicating "yes" or "no."

A Read the article. Then answer the questions.

1. What were these Americans doing in other countries? ....
2. What was Lisa trying to buy? ....
3. How do people show "yes" in Micronesia? ....
4. Who was Jan talking to? ....
5. What does a head nod mean in Bulgaria? ....
6. Why did Tom misunderstand his class? ....

B What do these words refer to? Write the correct word(s).

1. it (par. 1, line 2)   ....
2. their (par. 1, line 4)   ....
3. her (par. 2, line 8)   ....
4. that country (par. 3, line 6) ....
5. the same thing (par. 4, line 7) ....

C *Group work* Have you ever had a similar communication problem? What happened?

4 What a story!

SNAPSHOT

The Top Eight Newspaper Sections
Percent of adult U.S. newspaper readers who read each section

MAIN NEWS 70%

SPORTS 43%

EDITORIALS 42%

BUSINESS NEWS 39%

CLASSIFIED ADS 37%

COMICS 36%

MOVIE AND TV LISTINGS 33%

FOOD AND COOKING 32%

Source: Mediamark Research, Inc.

Which sections contain daily news? Which sections are for entertainment?
Put the sections in order from most interesting to least interesting.
What are two other sections or types of news stories that you like to read about?

2 **PERSPECTIVES** **A surprise ending**

A ▶ Listen to the TV news stories. What type of stories are they?

An attempted robbery took place at Eastern Bank today. A man was trying to rob the bank, but he wasn't very lucky! While he was escaping from the bank, the robber got caught in the revolving door. The police arrived and took the man to jail.

It was a strange soccer match last night. The Bears won the game, but the Lions scored the goal! As Jake Walters was running toward the ball, he tripped and accidentally kicked it into the wrong goal. The score was Bears 1, Lions 0.

An embarrassing incident happened at the Transportation Conference this morning. The Secretary of Transportation was making a speech when a protester threw an egg at her. The protester was arrested, and the secretary finished her speech.

An electrical problem at Pax Arena interrupted a Planets concert last night. The Planets were performing a new song when the lights went out. But the show went on! The Planets continued to play in the dark, and the lights came back on an hour later.

B *Pair work* What happened in each story to change the ending?

③ GRAMMAR FOCUS

Past continuous vs. simple past ▶

Use the past continuous for an ongoing action in the past.
Use the simple past for an event that interrupts that action.

Past continuous	Simple past
While he **was escaping** from the bank,	the robber **got caught** in the revolving door.
As Jake **was running** toward the ball,	he **tripped** and **kicked** it into the wrong goal.
The secretary **was making** a speech	when a protestor **threw** an egg at her.

A Complete the news stories using the past continuous and the simple past. Use the verbs given. Then compare with a partner.

DAILY ROUND-UP

Divers Hit the Jackpot!

While divers .... (work) off the coast of Florida, they .... (discover) a shipwreck containing gold worth $2 million. The divers .... (film) a show about the coral reef when they .... (find) the gold.

Four-legged Customers

As a woman .... (walk) her pet poodle down the street, a hair stylist .... (notice) them through the window and suddenly .... (have) a great idea. Later, while he .... (create) a new line of hair care products for dogs and cats, he .... (come up with) a new slogan: "Even animals have bad hair days!"

Rescue . . . the Ambulance!

An ambulance driver .... (have) breakfast in a coffee shop when a woman .... (hop) into his ambulance and .... (drive) away. The driver .... (hurry) to a phone and .... (alert) the police. The carjacker .... (go) over 90 miles an hour when the highway patrol finally .... (catch up with) her.

B *Group work* Take turns retelling the stories in part A. Try to add new information or think of a different ending to each story.

④ PRONUNCIATION Intonation in complex sentences

A ▶ Listen and practice. Notice how each clause in a complex sentence has its own intonation pattern.

While divers were working off the coast of Florida, they discovered a shipwreck.

As a woman was walking her pet poodle, a hair stylist noticed them through the window.

B *Pair work* Use your imagination to make complex sentences. Take turns starting and finishing the sentences. Pay attention to intonation.

A: While Sam was traveling in South America . . .
B: . . . he ran into an old friend in Lima.

5 LISTENING News broadcasts

A Listen to news broadcasts about three events. Do the stories have a happy ending? Take notes about each event.

Where did it happen?	When did it happen?	What happened?
1.		
2.		
3.		

B *Group work* Take turns describing each event in your own words.

6 SPEAKING That's incredible!

A *Group work* Match each headline with the beginning of a news story. Then choose one of the stories and make up more information. One student starts the story. Then another student tells what happened next, and so on.

1. ....
2. ....
3. ....
4. ....

ILLUSION OR ALIENS?

Identical Twins Reunited After 45 Years Apart

Man Receives Letter Mailed 50 Years Ago

Job Applicant's Life Saved by Being 5 Minutes Late

a. Rick Jones got a surprise when he went to his mailbox last week.

b. A strange light lit up the sky as three students were driving home last night.

c. Lisa Miller is lucky. As she was hurrying to a job interview, she missed her bus.

d. Ellen and Mary could hardly believe their eyes when they saw each other.

B *Class activity* Take turns telling the groups' stories. Other students ask questions. Which group has the best story?

7 WRITING A newspaper article

A Write a news story for one of the headlines in Exercise 6, or use your own idea. First, answer these questions. Then write your article.

Who was involved?   Where did it happen?   Why did it happen?
When did it happen?   How did it happen?   What was the outcome?

B *Pair work* Read your partner's story and ask questions to get more information. Then revise your article.

8 INTERCHANGE 4 A double ending

Solve a mystery! Go to Interchange 4.

9 CONVERSATION *What happened?*

A ▶ Listen and practice.

Brian: Someone stole my wallet last night!
Kathy: Oh no! What happened?
Brian: Well, I was working out, and I had put my
stuff in my locker, just like I always do.
When I came back, someone had stolen my
wallet. I guess I'd forgotten to lock the locker.
Kathy: That's terrible! Did you lose much money?
Brian: Only about $15. But I lost my credit card
and my driver's license. What a pain!

B ▶ Listen to the rest of the conversation. What did
Kathy have stolen once? Where was she? What happened?

10 GRAMMAR FOCUS

Past perfect ◐

*Use the past perfect for an event that occurred before
another event or time period in the past.*

Past event	Past perfect event
I **was working out**,	and I **had put** my stuff in my locker.
When I **came back**,	someone **had stolen** my wallet.
They **were able to** steal it	because I **had forgotten** to lock the locker.

A Complete the sentences. Use the simple past or past continuous with the
verbs in column A, and the simple past or the past perfect in column B.

A

1. A thief .... (break into) our house
last night while my sister and I ....
(pick up) a pizza for dinner.

2. I .... (shop) with some friends
yesterday, and I .... (lose) my keys.

3. I .... (drive) around with friends
all day on Sunday, and I ....
(run out) of gas on the freeway.

4. I .... (try) to go and visit my
parents last night when I ....
(get) stuck in the elevator in their
apartment building.

B

a. Luckily, I .... (give) a friend a copy of
them, and she .... (come over) and let
me into my apartment.

b. It .... (reach) the fifth floor when
it .... (stop). After I .... (be) stuck
for an hour, someone .... (start) it again.

c. I guess we .... (leave) the door unlocked
because that's how the thief .... (get)
into the house.

d. Luckily, I .... (bring) my cell phone with
me, so I .... (call) my brother for help.

B Match columns A and B to make complete stories. Then add one more
sentence to each story. Take turns reading your stories with a partner.

11 WORD POWER Events

A Match the words in column A with the definitions in column B.

A   B

1. coincidence ....   a. an unexpected event that brings good fortune
2. disaster ....   b. a difficult situation with no obvious solution
3. emergency ....   c. something puzzling or unexplained
4. lucky break ....   d. an event that causes a lot of suffering or destruction
5. misfortune ....   e. a great success or achievement
6. mystery ....   f. unexpected events that seem to be connected
7. predicament ....   g. a sudden event requiring quick action
8. triumph ....   h. an unlucky event

B *Pair work* Choose three of the words from part A. Write situations for each word.

> *While two people were traveling separately in China, they met by chance at a restaurant in Shanghai. Even though they had both lived in the same town their whole lives, they had never met before. (coincidence)*

C *Group work* Read your situations in groups. Can others guess which word each situation describes?

12 SPEAKING Tell me more.

A *Pair work* Complete the stories. Then join another pair and compare stories.

> *"What a lucky break! I had just arrived at work when the mail room attendant handed me an envelope . . ."*

> *"What a mystery! I found a huge package on my doorstep one evening. I was surprised because I hadn't ordered anything, and . . ."*

B *Group work* Have you ever . . . ?

found yourself in a predicament   had an emergency
been unable to solve a mystery   had a lucky break

Tell the group about it and answer their questions.

A: I found myself in quite a predicament last week.
B: Really? What happened?
A: I had just sat down to dinner with my girlfriend when my father called to tell me I was late to my sister's graduation!
C: What did you do?

Strange but True –

Stories from the hottest tabloids in town

Look at the first paragraph below. What kinds of stories can you find in tabloid newspapers?
■ informative ■ newsworthy ■ unbelievable ■ entertaining ■ shocking ■ frightening

Tabloids are newspapers that specialize in news about people. The stories are often sensational and leave the reader wondering, "Could this really be true?"

Brasília, Brazil After Gilberto Carvalho – a million-dollar lottery winner – told reporters that his luck had come from a particular fish in a park pond, more than 200 other Brazilians spoke up with similar stories. They had rubbed this fish and soon after had won a prize! Although this "magic fish" is now under study and off-limits to the public, many people have won money simply by rubbing its picture.

Cleveland, Ohio, U.S. Bruce Zalmer, 32, is literally fireproof. His skin can withstand flames without pain or damage. And his lungs can take in oxygen from smoky air. Medical scientists are amazed that a human could have either of these qualities, let alone both. Although Zalmer sees himself as "just a regular guy," he once rescued a family of four from a burning building after firefighters had given up hope.

Nakuru, Kenya As tourists looked on in amazement, a spaceship kidnapped 11 elephants from a game preserve. The driver had stopped at a watering hole and the tourists were watching the elephants when a gigantic spaceship appeared. The ship shot down a powerful beam of orange light that sucked up the elephants and then flew off. Park officials confirmed that 11 full-grown elephants had disappeared.

Monterrey, Mexico Astounded doctors say that hundreds of people who had been old and sick became

young and healthy again by drinking from a water fountain in a public park. Park officials removed the fountain because crowds were becoming a danger. Yet the people who had drunk its water remained young and healthy – and made others young and healthy, too, simply by hugging them!

A Read the article. Find the words in *italics* in the article. Then check (✓) the meaning of each word.

1. *off-limits*   ☐ forbidden   ☐ without restrictions
2. *literally*   ☐ without truth   ☐ exactly as stated
3. *withstand*   ☐ accept or give in   ☐ bear or resist
4. *look on*   ☐ watch without participating ☐ watch with pleasure
5. *shoot down*   ☐ destroy with gunfire   ☐ send suddenly
6. *astounded*   ☐ very surprised   ☐ speechless

B Match the clauses in column A with information in column B. Then compare with a partner and take turns retelling the stories.

A

1. After people had rubbed the fish, ...
2. After the firefighters had given up hope, ...
3. After the driver had stopped for the tourists, ...
4. After people had drunk from the fountain, ...

B

a. they became young and healthy.
b. the elephants were kidnapped.
c. Zalmer was able to save the family.
d. they won money or other prizes.

C *Group work* Do you like to read tabloids? Why or why not?

Units 3-4 Progress check

SELF-ASSESSMENT

How well can you do these things? Check (✓) the boxes.

I can	Very well	OK	A little
Make requests with modals, *if* clauses, and gerunds (Ex. 1)	☐	☐	☐
Pass on messages using indirect requests (Ex. 2)	☐	☐	☐
Tell a story using the past continuous and simple past (Ex. 3)	☐	☐	☐
Listen to and understand sequence in the past (Ex. 4)	☐	☐	☐
Describe events using the past perfect (Ex. 5)	☐	☐	☐

1 ROLE PLAY I wonder if you'd . . .

Student A: You are planning a class party at your house. Think of three things you need help with. Then call a classmate and ask for help.

Student B: Student A is planning a party. Agree to help with some things, but not everything.

"Hi, Dave. I'm calling about the party. I wonder if you'd mind . . ."

Change roles and try the role play again.

2 DISCUSSION Mystery messages

A *Group work* Take turns reading each request. Then discuss the questions and come up with possible answers.

> I'm sorry to bother you, Ms. Collins, but if Mr. Wall in Apartment 213 uses my space again, I'll call a tow truck.

> I'd really like to borrow it for the match on Friday. Please tell Tom to let me know soon if it's OK.

> Tell your officers that she's brown and has a red collar. She answers to the name "Lady." Please call if you find her.

1. What is the situation?
2. Who is the request for? Who received the request and passed it on?
3. Write an indirect request for each situation.

"Please tell Mr. Wall . . ."

B *Class activity* Compare your answers. Which group has the most interesting answers for each message?

3 SPEAKING *What happened?*

A *Pair work* Choose a type of event from the box. Then make up a title for a story about it. Write the title on a piece of paper.

> disaster   emergency   lucky break   mystery   triumph

B *Pair work* Exchange titles with another pair. Discuss the questions *who*, *what*, *where*, *when*, *why*, and *how* about the other pair's title. Then make up a story.

C Share your story with the pair who wrote the title.

> *Dog Show Disaster*
>
> My brother recently entered his pet, Poofi, in a dog show. But Poofi is a cat! He was bringing Poofi into the show when . . .

4 LISTENING *What comes first?*

 Listen to each situation. Number the events from 1 to 3.

1. ☐ She hurt her ankle.   ☐ She was running.   ☐ She went to work.
2. ☐ John wrote me.   ☐ I didn't get the letter.   ☐ I moved away.
3. ☐ I was very scared.   ☐ The plane landed.   ☐ I was relieved.
4. ☐ His sister called.   ☐ He was taking a shower.   ☐ He turned on his answering machine.

5 DISCUSSION *From A to B*

Group work Choose the beginning of a story from column A and an ending from column B. Discuss interesting or unusual events that could link A to B. Then make up a story.

A: Once, I . . .

received an unexpected phone call.
was asked for an unusual favor.
accepted an interesting invitation.
owed someone a big apology.

B: Believe it or not, . . .

I opened the door, and a horse was standing there!
when I got there, everyone had left.
he didn't even remember what I had done.
it was the Prince of Wales!

A: Once, I received an unexpected phone call.
B: Let's see . . . I was making coffee when the phone rang.
C: It was early in the morning, and I had just gotten up.
D: I had not completely woken up yet, but . . .

WHAT'S NEXT?

Look at your Self-assessment again. Do you need to review anything?

5 Crossing cultures

1 WORD POWER Culture shock

A These words are used to describe how people sometimes feel when they live in a foreign country. Which are positive (**P**)? Which are negative (**N**)?

anxious ....
comfortable ....
confident ....
curious ....
depressed ....

embarrassed ....
enthusiastic ....
excited ....
fascinated ....
homesick ....

insecure ....
nervous ....
uncertain ....
uncomfortable ....
worried ....

anxious

B *Group work* Do you live (or would you like to live) in a foreign country? How did you feel (or would you feel) about moving there?

"I think I'd be nervous and feel a little uncertain, but I'd be enthusiastic, too!"

2 PERSPECTIVES If I moved to a foreign country . . .

A ▶ Listen to the people talk about moving to a foreign country. Would you have any of the same concerns?

.... "One thing I'd really miss is my mom's cooking."
.... "I'd be uncertain about the local food. I might not like it."
.... "Getting used to different customs might be difficult at first."
.... "My room at home is the thing that I'd miss the most. I'd be homesick."
.... "Communicating in a new language is something I'd be anxious about."
.... "Moving to a country with a very different climate could be a challenge."
.... "I'd be worried about getting sick and not knowing how to find a good doctor."
.... "Something I'd be nervous about is making new friends, especially in a foreign language."

B Rank each concern in part A from 1 to 5. What is your biggest concern? Tell the class.

1 = Confident. I wouldn't be worried about this at all.
2 = Comfortable. I think this would be OK.
3 = Uncertain. This might be a problem for me.
4 = Insecure. This would make me nervous.
5 = Anxious. I would really be uncomfortable about this.

③ GRAMMAR FOCUS

Noun phrases containing relative clauses ▶

As a subject

One thing (that) I'd really miss is my mom's cooking.

Something (that) I'd be nervous about is making new friends.

Two people (who/that) I'd e-mail every day are my parents.

As an object

My mom's cooking is **one thing (that) I'd really miss.**

Making new friends is **something (that) I'd be nervous about.**

My parents are **two people (who/that) I'd e-mail every day.**

A Complete the sentences about living in a foreign country. Use the phrases below. Then compare with a partner.

my friends	trying new foods	making new friends	getting lost in a new city
my family	my favorite food	being away from home	not understanding people
getting sick	my room at home	speaking a new language	getting used to a different culture

1. One thing I'd definitely be fascinated by is . . .
2. . . . is something I'd really miss.
3. Two things I'd be homesick for are . . .
4. . . . are two things I'd be anxious about.
5. Something that would depress me is . . .
6. . . . is one thing that I might be embarrassed about.
7. The most uncomfortable thing would be . . .
8. . . . is something from home that I'd never miss.
9. One thing I'd be insecure about is . . .
10. . . . are two things I'd be very enthusiastic about.

B Now complete the sentences in part A with your own information.

C *Group work* Rewrite each sentence in another way. Then compare. Do others feel the same way?

> 1. Trying new foods is one thing
> I'd definitely be fascinated by.

④ PRONUNCIATION *Word stress in sentences*

A ▶ Listen and practice. Notice that the important words in a sentence have more stress.

Argentina is a country that I'd like to live in.

Speaking a new language is something I'd be anxious about.

B *Pair work* Mark the stress in the sentences you wrote in part A of Exercise 3. Then practice the sentences. Pay attention to word stress.

Crossing cultures • **31**

5 DISCUSSION Going abroad

Group work Read the questions. Think of two more questions to add to the list. Then take turns asking and answering the questions in groups.

If you could live in a foreign country, what country would you like to live in? Why?
What country wouldn't you like to live in? Why?
Who is the person you would most like to go abroad with?
What is something you would never travel without?
Who is the person you would e-mail first after arriving somewhere new?
What would be your two greatest concerns about living abroad?
What is the thing you would enjoy the most about living abroad?

A: What country would you like to live in?
B: The country I'd most like to live in is Bolivia.
C: Why is that?
B: Well, I've always wanted to learn about weaving. . . .

6 SNAPSHOT

Different Customs

Canada
If you are invited for a meal, you should arrive on time – not early or late.

Indonesia
Never point to anything with your foot.

France
When eating out, keep both hands on or above the table.

South Korea
Always use both hands to pass something to an older person.

Egypt
Don't eat anything with your left hand.

Thailand
Never touch anyone – especially a child – on the head.

Source: *Kiss, Bow, or Shake Hands*

Does your culture follow any of these customs?
Do any of these customs seem unusual to you? Explain.
What other interesting customs do you know?
What customs should a visitor to your country know about?

7 CONVERSATION What's the custom?

A ▶ Listen and practice.

Marta: Guess what! I just got invited to my teacher's house for dinner.
Karen: Oh, how nice!
Marta: Yes, but what do you do here when you're invited to someone's house?
Karen: Well, it's the custom to bring a small gift.
Marta: Really? Like what?
Karen: Oh, maybe some flowers or chocolates.
Marta: And is it all right to bring a friend along?
Karen: Well, if you want to bring someone, you're expected to call first and ask if it's OK.

B *Class activity* Are any of these customs the same in your country?

8 GRAMMAR FOCUS

Expectations ▶

When you visit someone,	it**'s the custom to** bring a small gift.
	you **aren't supposed to** arrive early.
If you want to bring someone,	you**'re expected to** call first and ask.
	you**'re supposed to** check with the host.
	it**'s not acceptable to** arrive without calling first.

A Match information in columns A and B to make sentences about customs in the United States and Canada. Then compare with a partner.

A

1. If you plan to visit someone at home, ...
2. If you've been to a friend's home for dinner, ...
3. When you have been invited to a wedding, ...
4. When you go out on a date, ...
5. If the service in a restaurant is good, ...
6. When you meet someone for the first time, ...

B

a. you're supposed to call first.
b. you're expected to leave a tip.
c. you aren't supposed to kiss him or her.
d. you're expected to respond in writing.
e. it's the custom to call and thank him or her.
f. it's acceptable to share the expenses.

B *Group work* How are the customs in part A different in your country?

C Complete these sentences with information about your country or a country you know well. Then compare with a partner.

1. In . . . , if people invite you to their home, . . .
2. When you go out with friends for dinner, . . .
3. If a friend gets engaged to be married, . . .
4. When a relative has a birthday, . . .
5. If a friend is in the hospital, . . .
6. When someone is going to have a baby, . . .

9 LISTENING Unique customs

▶ Listen to people describe customs they observed abroad. Complete the chart.

	Where was the person?	What was the custom?	How did the person react?
1. Alice			
2. John			
3. Susan			

10 SPEAKING Things to remember

Canadian doctor in Nepal

A *Pair work* What should a visitor to your country know about local customs? Make a list. Include these points.

dressing appropriately · giving and receiving gifts
staying in someone's home · taking photographs
traveling by bus or train · shopping

B *Class activity* Compare your lists around the class. Do any of your classmates' customs surprise you?

useful expressions
One of the most important things to remember is . . .
Another thing to keep in mind is . . .
One thing visitors often don't realize is . . .

11 WRITING A tourist pamphlet

A Choose five points from the list you made in Exercise 10. Use them to write a tourist pamphlet for your country.

Tips for Travelers

When you visit Indonesia, there are some important things you should know. For example, if you are visiting a mosque or temple, it's not acceptable to take photographs. Also, you are supposed to . . .

B *Pair work* Read your partner's pamphlet. Would a visitor to that country have all the information he or she needs?

12 INTERCHANGE 5 Culture check

Compare customs in different countries. Go to Interchange 5.

Culture Shock

Kit-ken Lim, a student from Taipei, Taiwan, is studying in Chicago. The following excerpts are taken from her journal during her first month in the United States.

What kinds of experiences can you gain from traveling to and living in other cities?

August 31
People often refer to Taipei as "The Sleepless City," but I didn't understand why until I got to Chicago. I was window-shopping with another student this evening when suddenly the store owners along the street started pulling down their gates and locking their doors. Soon the whole street was closed, even though it was still light out. This is something I've never seen in Taiwan, where the busiest streets "stay awake" all night. You can go out to restaurants, stores, and movies even long after midnight.

September 5
After the first week of class, I've found some differences between Taiwanese students and American students. Whenever a teacher asks a question, my classmates blurt out their answers almost immediately. And some of them interrupt the teacher. In Taipei, we're usually quiet in class so the teacher can finish on time. We tend to ask the teacher questions afterward. I don't know whether it's acceptable here for students to ask teachers questions after class.

October 6
I met a really interesting girl in my neighborhood café. I was writing a letter to my mother, and she asked me what language I was writing in. We ended up talking for about an hour! People in Chicago seem very comfortable with each other. It seems quite natural for two people to just start talking in a café. This is something that doesn't happen in Taipei. At home, I would never just start chatting with a stranger. I like that it's easy to meet new people here.

A Read the article. Then match each journal entry with its main idea.

1. August 31 ....   a. People in Taipei tend to be more private than in Chicago.
2. September 5 ....   b. Business hours in Chicago are much shorter than in Taipei.
3. October 6 ....   c. American students are more outspoken than Taiwanese students.

B Complete the chart.

	Chicago	Taipei
1. When does the city shut down?		
2. How do students behave in class?		
3. How do people act toward strangers?		

C *Pair work* How do things in your city compare with Taipei? with Chicago?

⑥ What's wrong with it?

1 SNAPSHOT

Some Common Complaints

Restaurants	Food stores	Cleaners	Doctors	Landlords	Taxis
Your food is undercooked.	You buy some milk. When you open it, you discover it has already gone sour.	The dry cleaner shrinks your favorite sweater.	You have to wait a long time for your doctor's appointment.	The sink is leaking, and your landlord won't fix it.	The driver tries to charge you too much.

Source: Based on information from *The Great American Gripe Book*

Have you ever had any of these complaints? Which ones?
What would you do in each of these situations?
What other complaints have you had?

2 PERSPECTIVES

A ▶ Listen to people describe complaints on a call-in radio show.

Ask Priscilla the Problem Solver!

1. "I ordered a jacket from a catalog, but when it arrived I found the lining was torn."
2. "I bought a new table from a store, but when they delivered it I noticed it was damaged on the top."
3. "A friend sent me a vase for my birthday, but when it arrived it was chipped."
4. "I took some pants to the cleaners, and when they came back they had a stain on them."
5. "I lent a friend my sunglasses, and now there are scratches on the lenses."
6. "I bought a nice aquarium a couple of weeks ago, but now it's leaking."

- [ ] ask for a refund
- [ ] ask the company to repair it
- [ ] ask for a discount
- [ ] ask the store to replace it
- [ ] tell her about it
- [ ] say nothing and repair it
- [ ] wash them by hand
- [ ] ask the cleaners to replace them
- [ ] say nothing
- [ ] ask him to replace them
- [ ] try fixing the leak
- [ ] take it back to the store

B Check (✓) what you think each person should do.

Describing problems 1 ◗

With past participles as adjectives	With nouns
The jacket lining is **torn**.	It has **a tear** in it. / There's **a hole** in it.
The tabletop is **damaged**.	There is **some damage** on the top.
That vase is **chipped**.	There is **a chip** in it.
My pants are **stained**.	They have **a stain** on them.
Her sunglasses are a little **scratched**.	There are **a few scratches** on them.
Their new aquarium **is leaking**.*	It has **a leak** in it.

A Read the comments from customers in a restaurant. Write sentences in two different ways using forms of the word in parentheses. Then compare with a partner.

1. This tablecloth isn't very clean. It's . . . (stain)
2. Could we have another water pitcher? This one . . . (leak)
3. The table looks pretty dirty. The wood . . . , too. (scratch)
4. The waiter needs a new shirt. The one he's wearing . . . (tear)
5. Could you bring me another cup of coffee? This cup . . . (chip)
6. The walls really need paint. And the ceiling . . . (damage)

B *Pair work* Describe two problems with each thing. Use the past participle, verb, or noun forms of the words in the box.

A: The mug is chipped.
B: Yes. And it has a crack on the side.

1. a mug

2. a pen

3. a CD

break
burn
chip
crack
dent
leak
scratch
stain
tear

4. a pair of glasses

5. a pair of jeans

6. a newspaper

C *Group work* Look around your classroom. How many problems can you describe?

"The floor is scratched, and the window is cracked. The desks are . . ."

LISTENING *Fair exchange?*

A Listen to three customers return an item they purchased.
What's the problem? Take notes. Then complete the chart.

Item	Problem	Will the store exchange it?	
		Yes	**No**
1.	....	☐	☐
2.	....	☐	☐
3.	....	☐	☐

B Were the solutions fair? Why or why not?

 ROLE PLAY *What's the problem?*

Student A: You are returning an item to a store. Decide
what the item is and explain why you are returning it.

Student B: You are a salesperson. A customer is
returning an item to the store. Ask these questions:

What exactly is the problem? Can you show it to me?
When did you buy the item? Was it like this when you
bought it? Do you have the receipt? Would you like
a refund or a store credit?

Change roles and try the role play again.

 **CONVERSATION** *It keeps burning!*

A Listen and practice.

Ms. Lock: Hello.
Mr. Burr: Hello, Ms. Lock. This is Jack Burr.
Ms. Lock: Uh, Mr. Burr . . .
Mr. Burr: In Apartment 305.
Ms. Lock: Oh, yes. What can I do for you? Does your
refrigerator need fixing again?
Mr. Burr: No, it's the oven this time.
Ms. Lock: Oh, so what's wrong with it?
Mr. Burr: Well, I think the temperature control needs
to be adjusted. The oven keeps burning
everything I try to cook.
Ms. Lock: Really? OK, I'll have someone look at it
right away.
Mr. Burr: Thanks a lot, Ms. Lock.
Ms. Lock: Uh, by the way, Mr. Burr, are you sure it's
the oven and not your cooking?

B Listen to another tenant calling Ms. Lock. What's the tenant's problem?

7 GRAMMAR FOCUS

Describing problems 2 ▶

Keep + gerund	Need + gerund	Need + passive infinitive
Everything **keeps burning**.	The oven **needs adjusting**.	It **needs to be adjusted**.
The alarm **keeps going off**.	The alarm **needs fixing**.	It **needs to be fixed**.

A What needs to be done in this apartment? Write sentences about these items using *need* with gerunds or passive infinitives.

1. the walls   (paint)
2. the rug   (clean)
3. the windows   (wash)
4. the clothes   (pick up)
5. the lamp shade   (replace)
6. the wastebasket   (empty)
7. the ceiling fan   (adjust)
8. the plant   (water)

> The walls need to be painted.
> OR
> The walls need painting.

B *Pair work* Think of five improvements you would like to make in your home. Which improvements will you most likely make? Which won't you make?

"First, the fire alarm in the kitchen needs replacing. It keeps going off. . . ."

8 WORD POWER Electronics

A Complete the sentences using the correct form of *keep* plus the correct form of the words in the box. Then compare with a partner. (More than one answer is possible.)

1. My computer is driving me crazy! It . . .
2. The buttons on the remote control always stick. They . . .
3. That used CD player often jumps to another song. It . . .
4. Our new flat-screen TV has a problem. It . . .
5. Those old cell phones never work right anymore. They . . .
6. Sometimes Ed can't use his solar-powered calculator. It . . .
7. My computer screen needs to be replaced. It . . .
8. The answering machine never picks up any calls. It . . .

break down
crash
flicker
freeze
go dead
jam
overheat
skip

B *Group work* Describe a problem with an electronic item you own. Don't identify it! Others will try to guess the item.

"Something I own keeps jamming. It happens when I'm driving. . . ."

9 PRONUNCIATION *Contrastive stress*

A ▶ Listen and practice. Notice how a change in stress changes the meaning of each question, and elicits a different response.

Is the bedroom window cracked? (No, the kitchen window is cracked.)

Is the bedroom window cracked? (No, the bedroom door is cracked.)

Is the bedroom window cracked? (No, it's broken.)

B ▶ Listen to the questions. Check (✓) the correct response.

1. a. Are my jeans torn?
   ☐ No, they're stained.
   ☐ No, your shirt is torn.

   b. Are my jeans torn?
   ☐ No, they're stained.
   ☐ No, your shirt is torn.

2. a. Is the computer going dead?
   ☐ No, it's crashing.
   ☐ No, the cell phone is going dead.

   b. Is the computer going dead?
   ☐ No, it's crashing.
   ☐ No, the cell phone is going dead.

10 LISTENING *Repair jobs*

▶ Listen to three people talk about their job. Complete the chart.

	What does this person repair?	What is the typical problem?
1. Joe		
2. Louise		
3. Sam		

11 WRITING *A letter of complaint*

A Imagine that you bought something that was damaged. You took it back, but the clerk refused to exchange it. Write a letter to the store's manager describing the problem and what needs to be done.

> Manager, Smith's Beauty Supply:
>
> A week ago I bought a hair dryer in your store. After using it three times, I discovered it was damaged. It keeps overheating and . . .

B *Group work* Read your classmates' letters. What would you do if you were the manager? Discuss other solutions to the problem.

12 INTERCHANGE 6 *Fixer-upper*

Do you have an eye for detail? Student A find Interchange 6A; Student B find Interchange 6B.

Trading Spaces

Skim the article. Why do you think the show is called Trading Spaces?

How fast can a home remodeling project be completed? About 48 hours. At least, that's the basis of the popular reality TV show called *Trading Spaces*.

Two sets of neighbors switch homes for two days and redecorate a single room in their neighbors' home. Both "teams" have the help of a designer, a handyman, and a budget of $1,000. At the end of the second day, the host reveals the rooms to the homeowners, who usually say, "Wow! That's great!" Sometimes, however, they get upset.

Is this reality TV realistic? Up to a point. The designers actually get videotapes of the rooms and plan out every step beforehand. Even the materials are purchased in advance. "It's the same at home," one designer said. "If you don't want a project to last for months, you need a game plan."

"Everybody thinks *Trading Spaces* is totally real, but *Trading Spaces* is totally not real,"

before

said a woman who appeared on the show. "If we didn't do [something on camera] right, we had to do it again. . . .You become an actor."

So, how happy are homeowners after their remodeling? Generally, the participants are thrilled. But one couple in Portland, Oregon, hated their new room. Their comfortable but cramped family room was transformed into a dark movie theater.

But you didn't see that on the show. "You didn't see me crying," said Shannon Pitts. They edited it out of the show.

"It really was a non-functional room," said Scott Pitts. "All you could do was watch TV." So they found themselves remodeling their own space again.

after

But even though Shannon and Scott didn't like the way their family room turned out, they'd still be on the show again. Why? They loved redecorating their neighbors' place.

A Read the article. Then for each statement, check (✓) True, False, or Not given.

	True	False	Not given
1. The participants of the show get assistance from experts.	☐	☐	☐
2. The projects sometimes take months to complete.	☐	☐	☐
3. Many participants redecorate their homes after the show.	☐	☐	☐
4. The people who appear on the show are actors.	☐	☐	☐
5. Reality shows aren't always entirely honest.	☐	☐	☐
6. The Pitts are no longer friends with their neighbors.	☐	☐	☐

B Check (✓) the statements the writer would probably agree with.

☐ 1. *Trading Spaces* needs to be more truthful about what happens behind the scenes.

☐ 2. *Trading Spaces* is a successful show, so they don't need to change anything.

☐ 3. *Trading Spaces* isn't always honest, but the participants still enjoy the experience.

C *Group work* Would you agree to let someone redecorate your home? Why or why not?

Units 5-6 Progress check

SELF-ASSESSMENT

How well can you do these things? Check (✓) the boxes.

I can	Very well	OK	A little
Describe emotions using noun phrases containing relative clauses (Ex. 1)	☐	☐	☐
Talk about differences in customs and expectations (Ex. 2)	☐	☐	☐
Listen to and understand problems and complaints (Ex. 3)	☐	☐	☐
Describe problems using nouns and past participles as adjectives (Ex. 4)	☐	☐	☐
Describe problems using gerunds and passive infinitives (Ex. 5)	☐	☐	☐

1 SPEAKING How would you feel?

Pair work Take turns. Choose a situation. Then ask your partner questions using the words in the box.

getting married   starting a new job
meeting your hero   going to a new school

anxious	excited
curious	insecure
embarrassed	nervous
enthusiastic	worried

A: If you were getting married tomorrow, what would you be anxious about?
B: One thing I'd be anxious about is the vows. I'd be worried about saying the wrong thing!

2 SURVEY What's acceptable?

A What do you think of these behaviors? Complete the survey.

It's acceptable to	Yes	No	It depends
kiss in public	☐	☐	☐
ask how old someone is	☐	☐	☐
call your parents by their first names	☐	☐	☐
use a cell phone in a restaurant	☐	☐	☐
put your feet on the furniture	☐	☐	☐

B **Group work** Compare your opinions. When are these behaviors acceptable? When are they unacceptable? What behaviors are never acceptable?

A: It's not acceptable to kiss in public.
B: Oh, I think it depends. In my country, if you're greeting someone, it's the custom to kiss on the cheek.

3 LISTENING Complaints

A ▶ Listen to three tenants complain to their building manager. Complete the chart.

Tenant's complaints	How the problems are solved
1.	....
2.	....
3.	....

B *Group work* Do you agree with the solutions? How would you solve the problems?

4 ROLE PLAY Haggling

Student A: Imagine you are buying this car from Student B, but it's too expensive. Describe the problems you see to get a better price.

Student B: You are trying to sell this car, but it has some problems. Make excuses for the problems to get the most money.

A: I want to buy this car, but the body has a few scratches. I'll give you $ . . . for it.
B: That's no big deal. You can't really see them, anyway. How about $ . . . ?
A: Well, what about the seat? It's . . .
B: You can fix that easily. . . .

Change roles and try the role play again.

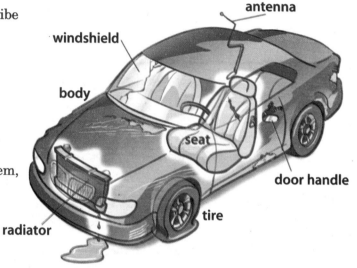

5 DISCUSSION School council meeting

A *Group work* Imagine you are on the school council. You are discussing improvements to your school. Decide on the five biggest issues.

A: The cafeteria food needs to be improved.
B: Yes, but it's more important to fix the computer in the lounge. It keeps crashing.

B *Class activity* Share your list with the class. What are the three most needed improvements? Can you think of how to accomplish them?

WHAT'S NEXT?

Look at your Self-assessment again. Do you need to review anything?

7 The world we live in

1 SNAPSHOT

WASTE NOT, WANT NOT *Some alarming facts*

In his or her lifetime, the average American born in the 1990s will . . .

- wear and throw away **115 pairs of shoes and boots**
- throw away **27,500 newspapers** – about **seven trees** a year
- use more than **28,000 gallons (106,000 liters) of gasoline**
- create over **110,000 pounds (50,000 kilograms) of trash**
- use **80–100 gallons (303–378 liters) of water** every day

Source: *Life's Big Instruction Book*; The Stevens Institute of Technology

Which of the things above seem the most wasteful?
How many pairs of shoes do you think you use every year? how many newspapers?
What are two other environmental problems that concern you?

2 PERSPECTIVES *Clean up our city!*

A ▶ Listen to an announcement from an election campaign.
What kinds of problems does Roberta Chang want to fix?

VOTE FOR ROBERTA CHANG * CITY COUNCIL
Roberta Chang will clean up Cradville!
Have you noticed these problems in our city?

- The air is being polluted by fumes from cars and trucks.
- The roadways have been jammed because of people's dependence on cars.
- Our city streets are being damaged as a result of heavy traffic.

- Many parks have been lost through overbuilding.
- The homeless have been displaced from city shelters due to overcrowding.
- Our fresh water supply is being depleted through overuse by people who don't conserve.

If you vote Roberta Chang for city council, you vote for solutions!

B Which of these problems affect your city? Can you give specific examples?

Passive with prepositions ○

Present continuous passive

The air **is being polluted** **by** fumes from cars and trucks.

City streets **are being damaged** **as a result of** heavy traffic.

Present perfect passive

The roadways **have been jammed** **because of** people's dependence on cars.

Many parks **have been lost** **through** overbuilding.

The homeless **have been displaced** **due to** overcrowding in city shelters.

A *Pair work* Match the photographs of environmental problems with the sentences below.

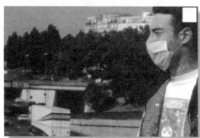  

1. Air pollution is threatening the health of people in urban areas.   (by)
2. Livestock farms have contaminated soil and underground water.   (because of)
3. The burning of gas, oil, and coal has created acid rain.   (as a result of)
4. The use of CFCs in products like hair spray has created a hole in the ozone layer.   (through)
5. The destruction of rain forests is harming rare plants and wildlife.   (through)
6. The growth of suburbs has eaten up huge amounts of farmland.   (due to)

B Rewrite the sentences in part A using the passive and the prepositions given. Then compare with a partner.

1. The health of people in urban areas is being threatened by air pollution.

C *Group work* Can you think of other causes for any of the problems above?

"The health of people in urban areas is also being threatened by contaminated water."

PRONUNCIATION *Reduction of auxiliary verbs*

A Listen and practice. Notice how the auxiliary verb forms **is**, **are**, **has**, and **have** are reduced in conversation.

Fresh water *is* being wasted.   Too much trash *has* been created.
Newspapers *are* being thrown away.   Parks *have* been lost.

B *Pair work* Practice the sentences you wrote in part B of Exercise 3. Pay attention to the reduction of **is**, **are**, **has**, and **have**.

5 **LISTENING** *Environmental solutions*

A Listen to three people describe some serious environmental problems. Write each problem in the chart.

	Problem	What can be done about it?
1. Jenny	....	....
2. Adam	....	....
3. Katy	....	....

B Listen again. What can be done to solve each problem? Complete the chart.

6 **WORD POWER** *World problems*

A *Pair work* How concerned are you about these problems? Check (✓) the appropriate box.

Problems	Very concerned	Fairly concerned	Not concerned
drug trafficking	☐	☐	☐
famine	☐	☐	☐
global warming	☐	☐	☐
government corruption	☐	☐	☐
HIV/AIDS	☐	☐	☐
inflation	☐	☐	☐
overpopulation	☐	☐	☐
political unrest	☐	☐	☐
poverty	☐	☐	☐

an AIDS awareness project

B *Group work* Join another pair. Which problems concern your group the most? What will happen if the problem isn't solved?

A: We need to educate more people about HIV/AIDS.
B: I agree. If we don't, the disease will continue to spread.
C: Yes. Many lives have been lost to due to . . .

7 CONVERSATION *What can we do?*

A ▶ Listen and practice.

Carla: Look at all those dead fish! What do you think happened?
Andy: Well, there's a factory outside town that's pumping chemicals into the river.
Carla: How can they do that? Isn't that against the law?
Andy: Yes, it is. But a lot of companies ignore those laws.
Carla: That's terrible! What can we do about it?
Andy: Well, one thing to do about it is to talk to the company's management.
Carla: What if that doesn't work?
Andy: Well, then another way to stop them is to get a TV station to run a story on it.
Carla: Yes! Companies hate bad publicity. By the way, what's the name of this company?
Andy: It's called Apex Industries.
Carla: Oh no! My uncle is one of their top executives!

B *Class activity* What else could Andy and Carla do?

C ▶ Listen to the rest of the conversation. What do Andy and Carla decide to do?

8 GRAMMAR FOCUS

> ### Infinitive clauses and phrases ▷
>
> One thing **to do about it** is **to talk to the company's management.**
> Another way **to stop them** is **to get a TV station to run a story.**
> The best ways **to fight HIV/AIDS** are **to do more research and educate people.**

A Find one or more solutions for each problem. Then compare with a partner.

Problems

1. One way to reduce famine is ....
2. The best way to fight HIV/AIDS is ....
3. One way to stop political unrest is ....
4. One thing to improve air quality is ....
5. The best way to reduce poverty is ....
6. One thing to help the homeless is ....

Solutions

a. to build more public housing.
b. to train people in modern farming methods.
c. to start free vocational training programs.
d. to educate people on how diseases are spread.
e. to have more police on the streets.
f. to provide ways for people to voice their concerns.
g. to develop cleaner public transportation.
h. to create more jobs for the unemployed.

B *Group work* Can you think of two more solutions for each problem in part A? Agree on the best solution for each.

9 DISCUSSION Problems and solutions

A *Pair work* Describe the problems shown in the photos.
Then make suggestions about how to solve these problems.

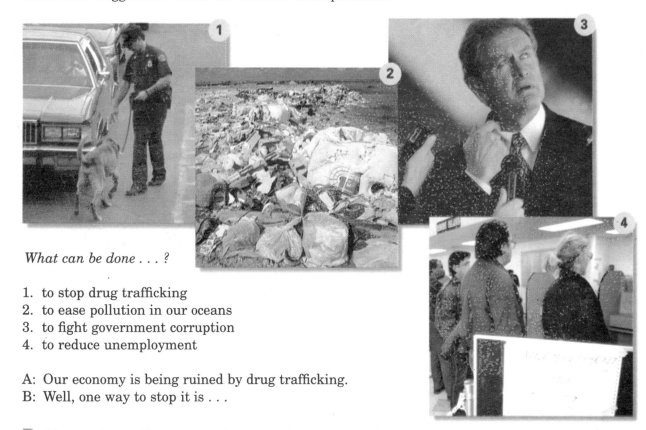

What can be done . . . ?

1. to stop drug trafficking
2. to ease pollution in our oceans
3. to fight government corruption
4. to reduce unemployment

A: Our economy is being ruined by drug trafficking.
B: Well, one way to stop it is . . .

B *Class activity* Share your solutions. Which ones
are the most innovative?

10 INTERCHANGE 7 Make your voices heard!

Brainstorm solutions to some local problems. Go to Interchange 7.

11 WRITING A letter to the editor

A Choose a problem from the unit or use one of your own ideas. Write a letter
to the editor of your newspaper describing the problem and one solution.

> Editor, the *Chronicle*,
>   Recently, poor farmers in our region have started growing
> poppies to earn money. Poppies produce opium, which is used to
> make illegal drugs. This has to stop!
>   One way to stop it is . . .

B *Pair work* Exchange letters with a partner. Write a response from the editor
suggesting another solution.

The Threat to KIRIBATI

Look at the picture. What do you think the threat to Kiribati might be?

The people of Kiribati (pronounced Kir-uh-bas) are afraid that one day in the near future, their country will disappear – literally. Several times in the past few years, the Pacific island nation has been flooded by sudden high tides. These tides, which swept across the islands and destroyed houses, came when there was neither wind nor rain. The older citizens of Kiribati say this has never happened before.

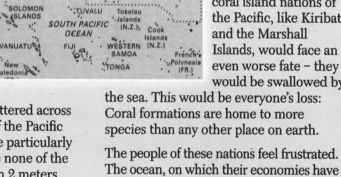

Kiribati consists of 33 islands scattered across 3,860 kilometers (2,400 miles) of the Pacific Ocean near the equator. They are particularly threatened by high tides because none of the islands of Kiribati rises more than 2 meters (6.5 feet) above sea level.

What is causing these mysterious tides? The answer may be global warming. When fuels like oil and coal are burned, they release pollutants that trap heat in the earth's atmosphere. Rising temperatures create more water by melting glaciers and polar ice caps.

Scientists say that if the trend continues, many countries will suffer. Bangladesh, for example, might lose one-fifth of its land. However, the coral island nations of the Pacific, like Kiribati and the Marshall Islands, would face an even worse fate – they would be swallowed by the sea. This would be everyone's loss: Coral formations are home to more species than any other place on earth.

The people of these nations feel frustrated. The ocean, on which their economies have always been based, is suddenly threatening their existence. There are no easy answers. These nations don't have a lot of money, so they can't afford expensive solutions, like sea walls. And they have no control over pollutants, which are being released mainly by large industrialized countries. All they can do is to hope that these countries will take steps to reduce pollution, and therefore, global warming.

A Read the article. Then complete the chart with information from the article.

Cause (Reason)		Effect (Result)
1. There have been sudden high tides.	→	*The island has been flooded.*
2.	→	Kiribati is particularly threatened by the tides.
3. Fuels like oil and coal are burned.	→	....
4.	→	Temperatures rise.
5.	→	The people of these nations feel frustrated.
6. Kiribati doesn't have a lot of money.	→	....

B *Group work* Some industrialized countries don't want to make changes until the effects of global warming are evident. What is your opinion? If you lived on an island like Kiribati, what would you like to see done?

8 Lifelong learning

1 SNAPSHOT

Popular College Majors

Broadcasting learn about television or radio media
Criminology study crime solving or prevention
Economics learn budgeting or international trade
Environmental Science study conservation or pollution
Exercise Science study fitness or sports management

Fashion learn design or merchandising
Film Studies study film history or film production
Hospitality study hotel or restaurant management
Interior Design decorate homes or buildings
Nutritional Science study children's nutrition or weight loss

Source: *http://www2.gasou.edu/sta/career/handouts.htm*

Which of these majors would be good for people who like to work with others?
for artistic types? for people who like to be outside? for problem solvers?
Which ones sound the most interesting to you? Why?

2 PERSPECTIVES

A ▶ Listen to a survey about adding courses to the curriculum.

CAMPUS SURVEY

We are expanding the school curriculum next year. What kinds of classes should we add? Please take a moment to answer a few questions.

1. Would you rather take a media class or a health class?
   ☐ a. I'd rather take a media class. (Go to question 2a.)
   ☐ b. I'd rather take a health class. (Go to question 2b.)
   ☐ c. I'd rather take another type of course than study media or health. (Go to question 3.)

2a. If you chose media class, would you prefer to study film studies or broadcasting?
   ☐ a. I'd prefer to study film studies.
   ☐ b. I'd prefer to study broadcasting.
   ☐ c. I'd prefer not to study either. I'd prefer another media course: _____

2b. If you chose health class, would you rather learn exercise science or nutritional science?
   ☐ a. I'd rather learn exercise science.
   ☐ b. I'd rather learn nutritional science.
   ☐ c. I'd rather not learn either. I'd prefer another health course: _____

3. What other types of courses would you add to the curriculum? _____

B Take the survey. Be sure to fill in the blanks if any of your answers are "c."

3 PRONUNCIATION *Intonation in questions of choice*

 Listen and practice. Notice the intonation in questions of choice.

Would you rather take broadcasting or economics?   Would you rather study fashion or hospitality?

Would you prefer to play the guitar or the violin?   Do you prefer to study in the day or at night?

4 GRAMMAR FOCUS

Would rather *and* would prefer ▶

Would rather takes the base form of the verb. Would prefer usually takes an infinitive. Both are followed by not *in the negative.*

Would you **rather take** a media class or a health class?
  I'**d rather take** a media class.
  I'**d rather not take** either.
  I'**d rather take** another course **than study** media or health.

Would you **prefer to study** film studies or broadcasting?
  I'**d prefer to study** film.   I'**d prefer not to study** either.

Let's join a choir.
  I'**d rather not join** a choir.
  I'**d rather not.**
  I'**d prefer not to join** a choir.
  I'**d prefer not to.**

A Complete the conversations with *would* and the appropriate form of the verbs in parentheses. Then practice with a partner.

1. A: .... you prefer .... a course in exercise science or nutritional science? (take)
   B: I'd prefer .... for a nutritional science course because it's more useful for me in nursing. (register)

2. A: .... you rather .... English in Australia or Canada? (learn)
   B: I think I'd prefer .... in Australia because it's warmer there. (study)

3. A: If you needed to learn a new skill, ... you prefer .... a class or .... a private tutor? (attend / have)
   B: I'd rather .... for a class than .... a tutor. Private tutors are too expensive! (sign up / hire)

4. A: .... you rather .... a choir or an orchestra? (join)
   B: I'd rather .... in a choir than .... in an orchestra. (sing / play)

5. A: .... you prefer .... broadcasting or film studies? (major in)
   B: To tell you the truth, I'd prefer not .... either. I'd rather .... for a newspaper. (do / work)

B *Pair work* Take turns asking the questions in part A. Pay attention to intonation. Give your own information when responding.

Lifelong learning • **51**

5 LISTENING *Just for fun*

A ▶ Listen to three people talk about the part-time courses they took recently. What course did each person take?

	What course each person took	What each person learned
1. Linda	....	....
2. Rich	....	....
3. Gwen	....	....

B ▶ Listen again. What additional information did each person learn?

6 ROLE PLAY *Choose a major.*

Student A: Look at the Snapshot on page 50 and choose a major. Tell Student B your major and explain why it's the right choice.

Student B: You are Student A's counselor. Convince Student A that he or she has made a bad choice. Give reasons why the major isn't right.

Change roles and try the role play again.

7 INTERCHANGE 8 *Learning curves*

What would your classmates like to learn? Take a survey. Go to Interchange 8.

8 CONVERSATION *Maybe I should try that!*

A ▶ Listen and practice.

Won Gyu: So how's your French class going?
    Kelly: Not bad, but I'm finding the pronunciation difficult.
Won Gyu: Well, it takes a while to get it right. You could improve your accent by listening to language CDs.
    Kelly: That's a good idea. But how do you learn new vocabulary? I always seem to forget new words.
Won Gyu: I learn new English words best by writing them on pieces of paper and sticking them on things in my room. I look at them every night before I go to sleep.
    Kelly: Hmm. Maybe I should try something like that!

B ▶ Listen to two other people explain how they learn new words in a foreign language. What techniques do they use?

C *Class activity* How do you learn new words in a foreign language?

9 GRAMMAR FOCUS

By + gerund to describe how to do things ○

You could improve your accent **by listening** to language CDs.
I learn new words best **by writing** them on pieces of paper and **sticking** them on things.
The best way to learn slang is not **by reading** newspapers but **by watching** movies.

A Complete the phrases in column A with information in column B.
(More than one answer is possible.) Then compare with a partner.

A

1. You can improve your accent ....
2. A good way to learn idioms is ....
3. Students can become better writers ....
4. A good way to learn new vocabulary is ....
5. People can become faster readers ....
6. One way of practicing conversation is ....
7. You can learn to use grammar correctly ....
8. The best way to develop self-confidence in speaking English is ....

B

a. by doing translation exercises.
b. by talking to native English speakers.
c. by reading magazines in English.
d. by studying a "learner's dictionary."
e. by role-playing with a partner.
f. by watching American movies.
g. by having a private tutor.
h. by talking to yourself in the shower.
i. by writing to English-speaking pen pals.
j. by joining a café conversation group.

B *Group work* Complete the phrases in column A with your own ideas.
Then compare. What's the best suggestion for each item?

A: In my opinion, a good way to improve your accent is by watching American sitcoms.
B: I think the best way is not by watching TV but by talking to native speakers.

10 DISCUSSION Ways of learning

A ▶ First, discuss how *you* would learn to do the things in the chart. Then listen
to Todd and Lucy describe how *they* developed these skills. How did they learn?

	Todd	Lucy
1. become a good cook		
2. become a good conversationalist		

B *Group work* Talk about the best ways to learn each of
these activities. Then agree on the most effective method.

better
ride a motorcycle
write a short story
use a new software program
play a musical instrument
be a good public speaker

11 WORD POWER Personal qualities

A *Pair work* How do we learn each of these things? Check (✓) your opinions. Then think of three other things we learn from our parents, from school, and on our own.

	From parents	From school	On our own
artistic appreciation	☐	☐	☐
communication skills	☐	☐	☐
competitiveness	☐	☐	☐
concern for others	☐	☐	☐
cooperation	☐	☐	☐
courtesy	☐	☐	☐
creativity	☐	☐	☐
perseverance	☐	☐	☐
self-confidence	☐	☐	☐
tolerance	☐	☐	☐

B *Group work* How can you develop each personal quality in part A? Use the activities listed in the box or your own ideas.

A: You can learn artistic appreciation by going to museums.
B: You can also learn it by studying painting or drawing.

some activities

studying world religions
volunteering in a hospital
taking a public speaking class
performing in a play
going to museums
learning a martial art
playing a team sport

12 WRITING A short speech

A Think of a skill, hobby, or craft you have learned. Read these questions and make notes. Then use your notes to write a short speech.

What is required to be successful at it?
What are some ways people learn to do it?
How did you learn it?
What was difficult about learning it?

> I enjoy cooking, and many people say I am a good cook. To be a good cook, you need both creativity and self-confidence. You need creativity to combine ingredients in new ways. . . .
>
> Some people learn to cook by taking classes or by following recipes in a cookbook. I first learned how to cook by watching my mother and helping her in the kitchen. Then . . .

B *Group work* Take turns giving your talks. Did your classmates' speeches inspire you to learn a new skill?

Learning Styles

Have you ever had trouble learning something? Did you overcome the problem? How?

Have you ever sat in class wondering if you would ever grasp the information that was being taught? Maybe the presentation didn't fit your learning style.

Our minds and bodies gather information in different ways and from all around us: seeing, hearing, and doing. Then our brains process that information, organizing it and making connections to things we already know. This process can also work in different ways: Do we think in pictures or words? Do we remember details or the big picture?

When we're trying to learn, it helps to know how our brain works. How do we best gather and organize information? Different people have different learning styles. For example, one person might struggle with written information but understand it immediately in an illustration. Another person might have problems with the picture, but not the written text.

Psychologists have identified seven basic learning styles:

Linguistic These people learn by using language – listening, reading, speaking, and writing.

Logical These people learn by applying formulas and scientific principles.

Visual These people learn by seeing what they are learning.

Musical Instead of finding music a distraction, these people learn well when information is presented through music.

Kinesthetic Movement and physical activities help these people learn.

Intrapersonal These people learn best if they associate new information directly with their own experiences.

Interpersonal These people learn well by working with others.

You will often encounter situations that do not match your strongest learning style. If you know what your strengths are, you can develop strategies to balance your weaknesses, for a more successful learning experience.

A Read the article. Find the words in *italics* in the article. Then match each word with its meaning.

.... 1. *grasp*   a. try hard to do something
.... 2. *the big picture*   b. understand
.... 3. *gather*   c. something that takes attention away
.... 4. *struggle*   d. show one thing is connected to another
.... 5. *distraction*   e. a general view of a situation
.... 6. *associate*   f. pick up or collect

B These sentences are false. Correct each one to make it true.

1. If you can't understand something, you aren't concentrating hard enough.
2. Linguistic learners will not comprehend written information.
3. A visual learner will probably learn best by listening and speaking.
4. A musical learner needs peace and quiet to focus on something.
5. Intrapersonal learners generally work well with other people.

C *Group work* Which learning styles work best for you?

Units 7–8 Progress check

SELF-ASSESSMENT

How well can you do these things? Check (✓) the boxes.

I can	Very well	OK	A little
Describe problems using the passive with prepositions (Ex. 1)	☐	☐	☐
Offer solutions with infinitive clauses and phrases (Ex. 2)	☐	☐	☐
Listen to and understand the meaning of personal qualities (Ex. 3)	☐	☐	☐
Ask about preferences using *would rather* and *would prefer* (Ex. 4)	☐	☐	☐
Talk about learning preferences with *by* + gerund (Ex. 4)	☐	☐	☐

1 GAME What's the cause?

Class activity Go around the room and make sentences. Check (✓) each phrase after it is used. The students who check the most items win.

Effect	Cause
☐ The quality of the air is being lowered	☐ heavy traffic
☐ Parks are being lost	☐ acid rain
☐ Water is being contaminated	☐ overbuilding
☐ Landfills are overflowing	☐ fumes from cars
☐ Forests are being damaged	☐ the lack of recycling
☐ City streets are being damaged	☐ factory waste

A: The quality of the air is being lowered . . .
B: . . . due to fumes from cars.

2 DISCUSSION Social disasters

A *Pair work* Read these problems that friends sometimes have with each other. Suggest solutions for each problem.

A friend is having a party and you weren't invited.
Your roommate keeps ruining your things.
Your friend always keeps you on the phone too long.

useful expressions
One thing to do is to . . .
Another way to help is to . . .
The best thing to do is . . .

B *Group work* Agree on the best solution for each problem.

"One thing to do is to ask a friend to talk to the host, to find out if it was a mistake."

3 LISTENING Personal qualities

 Listen to people talk about recent events and activities in their lives. What events and activities are they talking about? What quality does each person's behavior demonstrate? Complete the chart.

	Event or activity	Quality	
1. Mark	....	☐ competitiveness	☐ cooperation
2. Joan	....	☐ perseverance	☐ tolerance
3. Kim	....	☐ self-confidence	☐ creativity

4 QUESTIONNAIRE What works?

A *Pair work* What do you do to help improve your English? Interview a partner and circle his or her preferences.

Q&A

1. **When you make a mistake in English, would you prefer someone to . . .**
   (a) correct it immediately? *or* (b) ignore it?
2. **When you hear a new word in English, would you rather . . .**
   (a) write it down? *or* (b) try to remember it?
3. **If you don't understand what someone says, would you rather . . .**
   (a) ask the person to repeat it? *or* (b) pretend you understand?
4. **Would you prefer to speak English with . . .**
   (a) a native speaker? *or* (b) a non-native speaker?
5. **When you meet a native English speaker, . . .**
   (a) do you try to talk to the person? *or* (b) are you too shy to speak?
6. **When you use English and make mistakes, do you . . .**
   (a) let it bother you a lot? *or* (b) let it bother you only a little?

"I'd prefer someone to correct my mistakes immediately."

B *Group work* Discuss the advantages and disadvantages of each (a) or (b) option. Are there better options for each situation?

A: When someone corrects me immediately, I get nervous.
B: Yes, but when someone ignores the mistake, you don't know that you've made one.
C: I think the best way someone can help you is by correcting you at the end of a conversation.

WHAT'S NEXT?

Look at your Self-assessment again. Do you need to review anything?

9 At your service

1 ## SNAPSHOT

Eight commonly offered services

House painting

Pet-sitting

Language tutoring

House cleaning

Music lessons

Financial services

Essay typing

Handyman services

Source: Based on information from the community bulletin board at The Coffee Pot, New York City

Why would someone need these services? Have you ever used any of them?
What are some other common services and skills people offer?

2 ## PERSPECTIVES

A ▶ Listen to an advertisement for Hazel's Personal Services.
Would you use a service like this?

Hazel's Personal Services

Do you ever have questions like these?
- Where can I get my hair cut for a reasonable price?
- Do you know where I can have someone fix my bike?
- Where can I get someone to upgrade my computer?
- Do you know where I can have my leather jacket cleaned?

Do you know where you can have ALL these things done? Call Hazel! (646) 555-2121

Hazel offers
✓ Computer support
✓ Repairs
✓ Beauty services
✓ Financial services
✓ Laundry and dry cleaning
✓ Pet-sitting

If Hazel doesn't offer the service you need, she'll find someone who does. Guaranteed!

B What do you need to have done? What questions would you ask Hazel?

3 GRAMMAR FOCUS

Have or get something done ▶

Use have or get to describe a service performed for you by someone else.

Active

Do you know where I can **have** someone **fix** my bike?

    You can **have** Hazel's Personal Services **fix** your bike.

    You can **get** a repair shop **to fix** your bike.

Passive

Do you know where I can **have** my bike **fixed**?

    You can **have** your bike **fixed** by Hazel's Personal Services.

    You can **get** your bike **fixed** at a repair shop.

A Imagine you want to have someone do these things for you. Write questions using the active form of *have* or *get*.

I want to have someone / get someone to . . .

1. shorten my skirt
2. cut my hair
3. repair my watch
4. fix my scooter
5. take my passport photo
6. massage my neck
7. clean my leather jacket
8. take care of my pets while I'm away

> 1. Do you know where I can get someone to shorten my skirt?

B *Pair work* Take turns asking the questions. Answer using the passive with *have* or *get*.

A: Do you know where I can get someone to shorten my skirt?
B: You can have your skirt shortened at Main Street Cleaners.

4 PRONUNCIATION *Sentence stress*

A ▶ Listen and practice. Notice that when the object becomes a pronoun (sentence B), it is no longer stressed.

A: Where can I have someone **fix** my **watch**?

B: You can have someone **fix** it at the **Time** Shop.

A: Where can I have my **watch fixed**?

B: You can have it **fixed** at the **Time** Shop.

B *Group work* Ask questions about three things you want to have done. Pay attention to sentence stress. Other students give answers.

5 DISCUSSION Different places, different ways

Group work Are these services available in your country? For those that aren't, do you think they would be a good idea?

Can you . . . ?

have a suit or dress made on the street
have a meal served to you on a commuter bus
have your portrait drawn by a street artist
get your eyes examined in a shopping mall
get library books delivered to your home
check your e-mail in a bus terminal
do grocery shopping over the Internet
buy clothing from a vending machine

A: Can you have a suit made on the street here?
B: Sure! You can have it done lots of places downtown.

6 INTERCHANGE 9 Because I said so!

What do teenagers worry about? Go to Interchange 9 at the back of the book.

7 WORD POWER Three-word phrasal verbs

A Match each phrasal verb in these sentences with its meaning. Then compare with a partner.

Phrasal verbs

1. Jennifer has **broken up with** her boyfriend – again! ....
2. Kevin **came up with** a great idea for our class reunion. ....
3. I'm not **looking forward to** typing my essay. Maybe I'll get it done professionally. ....
4. My doctor says I'm overweight. I should **cut down on** fatty foods. ....
5. Rob can't **keep up with** the students in his Mandarin class. He should get a tutor. ....
6. I can't **put up with** the noise on my street! I'll have to move. ....
7. My girlfriend doesn't **get along with** her roommate. They're always fighting. ....
8. Bill can't **take care of** his own finances. He has an accountant manage his money. ....

Meanings

a. be excited for something to happen
b. end a romantic relationship
c. keep pace with someone or something
d. tolerate something you don't like
e. reduce the quantity of something
f. have a good relationship with someone
g. be responsible for something
h. think of something; develop an idea

B *Pair work* Take turns making sentences with each phrasal verb in part A.

8 CONVERSATION *I need a date!*

A ▶ Listen and practice.

James: This is so depressing! I haven't had a date since Angela broke up with me. What can I do?

Mike: What about looking through the personal ads on the Internet? That's how I met Amy.

James: Actually, I've tried that. But the people you meet are always different from what you expect.

Mike: Well, why don't you join an online dating service? A friend of mine met his wife that way.

James: That's not a bad idea.

Mike: Also, it might be a good idea to check out those discussion groups at the bookstore.

James: Yeah. If I don't meet someone, at least I might find a good book!

B *Class activity* What are some other good ways to meet people?

9 GRAMMAR FOCUS

Making suggestions ▶

With gerunds

What about looking through the personal ads?
Have you thought about joining . . . ?

With infinitives

It might be a good idea to check out those discussion groups at the bookstore.
One thing you could do is (to) go . . .

With modals + verbs

Maybe you could go to a chat room on the Internet.

With negative questions

Why don't you join a dating service?

A Match each problem below with the best suggestion. Then write sentences using the phrases in the grammar box. (More than one answer is possible.)

Problems

1. How can I build self-confidence? ....
2. What could help me be happier? ....
3. How can I lose weight? ....
4. What can I do to save money? ....
5. How can I improve my memory? ....
6. How can I get along with my roommate better? ....

Suggestions

a. cut down on calories
b. play concentration games
c. participate in more social activities
d. try not to get peeved about little things
e. come up with a budget
f. plan fun activities to look forward to every week

> *1. How can I build self-confidence? / One thing you could do is . . .*

B *Group work* Take turns asking and answering the questions in part A. What other suggestions can you think of for each problem?

10 *LISTENING* All you have to do is . . .

A ▶ Listen to three different suggestions for each problem in the chart. Write down the suggestion you think is best.

Problem	Best suggestion
1. how to overcome shyness	....
2. how to stop biting your fingernails	....
3. how to organize your busy schedule·	....

B *Group work* Compare your choices. Think of another suggestion for each problem.

11 *SPEAKING* Problems and solutions

Group work Give three suggestions for each of these problems. Then share your solutions with the class. Which solutions are the most creative?

How can I . . . ?

get in better shape

remember people's names more easily

learn to control my temper

"One thing you could do is join a gym. And what about cutting down on junk food?"

12 *WRITING* A letter of advice

A Imagine you are an advice columnist at a magazine. Choose one of the letters below and make a list of suggestions. Then write a reply.

My best friend seems anxious a lot. She bites her fingernails and looks tired all the time. I don't think she's eating right, either. How can I convince her to take better care of herself?

–Worried

I argue with my girlfriend all the time. I try to do nice things for her, but we always end up in a fight. I can't put up with this much longer – what can I do?

–Frustrated

B *Group work* Take turns reading your advice. Whose advice is best? Why?

Improve Your Memory, Improve Your Life

Have you ever been embarrassed because you forgot something important?
What kinds of things do you have the most trouble remembering?

- Mark began to introduce the guest speaker to the audience, but then paused in horror. He had forgotten her name.

- Barbara hid her jewelry when she went on vacation. When she came back, she couldn't remember where she'd put it.

1 Perhaps you've had experiences like these. Most people have. And, what's worse, most people have resigned themselves to a life of forgetting. They're unaware of a simple but important fact: Memory can be developed. If you'll just accept that fact, this book will show you how.

2 First, relax. If you're overanxious about remembering something, you'll forget it. Relaxing will enhance your awareness and ability to concentrate. Take

deep breaths and tell yourself that you have all the time in the world to remember.

3 Second, avoid being negative. If you keep telling yourself that your memory is bad, your mind will come to believe it and you won't remember things. When you forget something, don't say, "Gee, I need to have my

brain rewired." Jokes like this are negative and will have a negative effect on you and your memory.

4 To improve your memory, you'll need to take an active role. Like your body, your memory can be strengthened through exercise. Look for opportunities to exercise your memory. For example, if you're learning a language, try to actively remember irregular verbs.

5 You may also want to make associations, or links, between what you're trying to remember and things you already know. For example, if you need to catch a plane at 2:00 P.M., you can imagine a plane in your mind and notice that it has two wings. Two wings = 2:00. You are now ten times more likely to remember the take-off time.

A Read the article. Then write the number of each paragraph next to its main idea.

.... Your mind believes what you tell it, so be positive about your memory.
.... If you train your memory actively, you'll be more likely to remember things.
.... Although we all forget things, there are ways to improve our memory.
.... Learning to mentally connect pieces of information can help you remember.
.... We forget things more easily when we're worried about remembering them.

B Complete the chart.

General ways to improve memory	Specific examples of ways to improve memory
1. Relax	Take deep breaths; tell yourself you have time.
2.	
3.	
4.	

C *Group work* Which of the suggestions do you find the most useful? Why?

10 The past and the future

1 SNAPSHOT

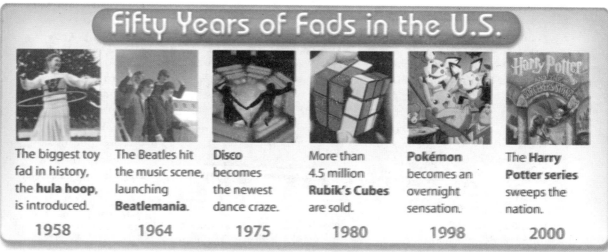

Fifty Years of Fads in the U.S.

The biggest toy fad in history, the **hula hoop**, is introduced.
1958

The Beatles hit the music scene, launching **Beatlemania**.
1964

Disco becomes the newest dance craze.
1975

More than 4.5 million **Rubik's Cubes** are sold.
1980

Pokémon becomes an overnight sensation.
1998

The **Harry Potter series** sweeps the nation.
2000

Sources: *New York Public Library Book of Chronologies; www.badfads.com; Pittsburgh Post-Gazette*

Have any of these fads ever been popular in your country?
Which of these fads would have interested you? Why?
Can you think of four other fads from the past or present?

2 CONVERSATION *I'm good at history.*

A ▶ Listen and practice.

Emma: Look. Here's a quiz on events of the twentieth century.

Steve: Oh, let me give it a try. I'm good at history.

Emma: All right. First question: When did World War I begin?

Steve: I think it began in 1917.

Emma: Huh. And how long has the United Nations been in existence?

Steve: Uh, since Kennedy became president in 1961.

Emma: Hmm. Next question: How long were the Beatles together?

Steve: Well, they started in 1965, and broke up in 1980, so they were together for 15 years. So, how am I doing so far?

Emma: Not very well. Not one of your answers is correct!

B ▶ Do you know the answers to the three questions in part A? Listen to the rest of the conversation. What are the correct answers?

64

③ GRAMMAR FOCUS

Referring to time in the past ◖

A point of time in the past
When did World War II take place?
During the 1940s. **In** the 1940s. Over 60 years **ago**.

A period of time in the past
How long were the Beatles together?
From 1960 **to** 1970. **For** ten years.

A period of time that continues into the present
How long has the United Nations been in existence?
Since 1945. **Since** World War II ended. **For** about the last 60 years.

A Complete the paragraphs with words from the grammar box. Then compare with a partner.

1. Rock music has been popular .... more than 50 years. The Beatles were a well-known English band .... the 1960s. They performed together .... ten years – .... 1960 .... 1970. In 2003, the Beatles released another album, even though two of the original members had already died. The album was recorded .... 1969, nearly 40 years ....

2. .... 2003, the United States launched two Mars exploration spacecraft. Their mission, which lasted .... more than a year, was to gather information about the rocks, soil, and atmosphere on Mars using rovers called *Spirit* and *Opportunity*. The rovers functioned longer than anyone expected – scientists thought they would last .... only four months on Mars. .... that time they have sent back thousands of live pictures of the surface of Mars.

B *Group work* Write two true and two false statements about world events. Then take turns reading your statements. Others give correct information for the false statements.

A: Disco has been popular since the 1940s.
B: That's false. It became popular during the 1970s.

The Beatles

Mars

④ PRONUNCIATION Syllable stress

A ◉ Listen and practice. Notice which syllable has the main stress in these four- and five-syllable words. Notice the secondary stress.

˯ ⊙ ˯ ˯
iden ti fy

˯ ˯ ⊙ ˯
disad van tage

˯ ˯ ˯ ⊙ ˯
communi ca tion

....

....

| appreciate |
| assassination |
| catastrophe |
| consideration |
| conversation |
| revolution |

B ◉ Listen to the words in the box. Which syllable has the main stress? Write the words in the correct column in part A.

5 WORD POWER Historic events

A Match each word with the best example. Then compare with a partner.

1. achievement ....
2. assassination ....
3. disaster ....
4. discovery ....
5. epidemic ....
6. invention ....
7. terrorist act ....

a. The luxury ship *Titanic* sank in the North Atlantic Ocean in 1912.
b. The cellular telephone was developed in Sweden about 25 years ago.
c. Four planes were hijacked in the United States on September 11, 2001.
d. In 2003, a dinosaur with feathers and four wings was found in China.
e. Since the late 1970s, HIV has infected an estimated 58 million people.
f. U.S. president John F. Kennedy was shot to death in 1963.
g. In 1953, Sir Edmund Hillary and the Sherpa Tenzing Norgay were the first to reach the summit of Mount Everest.

B *Pair work* Give another example for each word in part A.

"The exploration of Mars is an amazing achievement."

6 DISCUSSION It made a difference.

Group work Choose two or three historic events (a disaster, an epidemic, an invention, etc.) that had an impact on your country. Discuss the questions.

What happened (or what was achieved)? When did it happen?
What was the immediate effect on your country? the world? your family?
Did it change things permanently? How is life different now?

A: One disaster that occurs every three to five years is the weather condition called El Niño.
B: It affects the weather all over the world. It causes terrible flooding in South America.
C: Yes, and very dry weather in Southeast Asia. During one El Niño, in 1998, my grandmother in Indonesia lost her house due to fire.

7 WRITING A biography

A Find information about a person who has had a major influence on the world or your country. Answer these questions. Then write a biography.

What is this person famous for?
How and when did he or she become famous?
What are his or her important achievements?

B *Pair work* Exchange biographies. What additional details can your partner add?

Carter, Jimmy

Jimmy Carter first became famous as president of the United States from 1977 to 1981. Although he was not considered successful during his presidency, since he left office he has become well respected for his many achievements in human rights.

In 2002, he was awarded the Nobel Peace Prize for his efforts to find peaceful solutions to international conflicts and to promote economic and social development. . . .

8 INTERCHANGE 10 History buff

Find out how good you are at history. Go to the back of the book.
Student A find Interchange 10A; Student B find Interchange 10B.

9 PERSPECTIVES

A Listen to a survey about the future. Check (✓) the predictions you think will happen.

What will the future hold?

☐ Computers will recognize any voice command. You won't need a keyboard.

☐ Within 20 years, scientists will have discovered a cure for baldness.

☐ People will be living in cities under the ocean.

☐ By 2020, world leaders will have eliminated terrorism.

☐ Robots will be performing most factory jobs.

☐ By 2050, we will have set up human communities on Mars.

☐ Medical scientists will create an AIDS vaccine.

B Which of the predictions do you think will affect you?

10 GRAMMAR FOCUS

Predicting the future with will ▶

Use will to predict future events or situations.

Computers **will recognize** any voice command. You **won't need** a keyboard.

Use future continuous to predict ongoing actions.

People **will be living** in cities under the ocean.

Use future perfect to predict actions that will be completed by a certain time.

Within 20 years, scientists **will have discovered** a cure for baldness.
By 2050, we **will have set up** human communities on Mars.

A Complete these predictions with the correct verb forms. (More than one answer is possible.) Then compare with a partner.

1. In ten years, flights from New York to Tokyo .... less than two hours.   (take)

2. Soon they .... computers that can translate perfectly from one language to another.   (sell)

3. By the middle of the twenty-first century, scientists .... a way to prevent aging.   (discover)

4. Sometime in the future, scientists .... a machine that transmits our thoughts.   (invent)

5. Within 50 years, people .... on the moon.   (live)

6. In less than a century, global warming .... most of the polar ice caps and many coastal cities ....   (melt / disappear)

B *Group work* Discuss each prediction in part A. Do you agree or disagree?

A: In ten years, flights from New York to Tokyo will take less than two hours. What do you think?
B: Oh, I totally agree. I think they'll use space-shuttle technology to build faster airplanes.
C: I'm not so sure. Those flights normally take about 14 hours. How are they going to come up with an invention that shortens the trip by 12 hours?

C *Class activity* Discuss these questions.

1. What three recently developed technologies will have the greatest impact on our lives in the next 20 years?
2. What are the three most important changes that will have occurred on earth by 2050?
3. Which three jobs will people *not* be doing in 50 years? Why?

11 LISTENING *A perfect future?*

A Listen to people discussing changes that will affect these areas in the next 50 years. Write down two changes for each topic.

Future changes		
1. work	....	....
2. transportation	....	....
3. education	....	....
4. health	....	....

B *Group work* Can you suggest one more possible change for each area?

12 DISCUSSION *Things will be different!*

Group work Talk about these questions.

What do you think you'll be doing a year from now? five years from now?
Do you think you'll still be living in the same place?
What are three things you think you'll have accomplished within the next five years?
What are three things you won't have done within the next five years?
In what ways do you think you'll have changed by the time you retire?

THE GLOBAL VILLAGE

Scan the article. What does the term *global village* mean?

More and more often, the term *global village* is used to describe the world and its people. In most villages, everyone knows everyone else and the people face the same kinds of problems. So how can the world be a village when it is home to more than six billion people? Political and technological changes in the past century have made the global village possible.

POLITICAL CHANGES   The years following World War II seemed to promise peace. In fact, in 1945, the United Nations was founded to help countries resolve disputes peacefully. However, this promise was soon broken by the Cold War – distrust and tension between the United States and the Soviet Union. These two superpowers engaged in an arms race, spending huge amounts of money on weapons. The other nations of the world were divided into two "sides," and the world was frozen in a state of hostility.

The Cold War finally ended and the political climate changed between 1989 and 1991, when the governments of the Soviet Union and several Eastern European countries collapsed. The end of Cold War tension made the global village more politically possible by opening new channels of communication between nations.

TECHNOLOGICAL CHANGES   Technologically, the greatest contributor to the global village is the microchip – an electronic circuit on a tiny chip. The evolution of the microchip has made modern satellites and supercomputers possible. These forms of high-tech communications allow news and ideas to travel quickly across the globe, making people more aware of their neighbors around the world in dramatic new ways. Through the Internet, we can get information from computers and carry on electronic conversations with people everywhere. Through television programs transmitted by satellite, we are exposed to many cultures.

The development of the global village will almost certainly continue into the future. Not only is this probable, but the challenges that the world faces – for example, conflicts among peoples, pollution, and population growth – will make it necessary.

A Read the article. Then complete the summary with information from the article.

The term *global village* implies that people around .... are connected and face
.... The global village became possible because of .... and
.... changes in the past half century. Politically, the end of .... made
the global village possible by .... between nations. Technologically, the invention of
the .... has made .... and .... possible. These new
forms of communication have made people more aware of ....

B Use information in the article to answer the following questions in your own words.

1. What is the United Nations?
2. What was the Cold War?
3. Who were the superpowers?
4. What was the arms race?
5. What is a microchip?
6. What are high-tech communications?

C *Group work* What other challenges will the world face in the twenty-first century?

Units 9–10 Progress check

SELF-ASSESSMENT

How well can you do these things? Check (✓) the boxes.

I can	Very well	OK	A little
Talk about things people have or get done using the active and passive (Ex. 1)	☐	☐	☐
Make suggestions using a variety of structures (Ex. 2)	☐	☐	☐
Listen to, understand, and refer to time in the past (Ex. 3)	☐	☐	☐
Predict the future with *will*, future continuous, and future perfect (Ex. 4)	☐	☐	☐

1 DISCUSSION *Once in a while*

Group work Take turns asking questions about these services. When someone answers "yes," find out **why** and **when** the service was performed, and **who** performed it.

have a photo taken professionally
get someone to paint an apartment
get flowers delivered
have someone type an essay
get something translated

A: Has anyone ever had a photo taken professionally?
B: Yes, I have. I had it taken a few months ago.
C: Really? Why did you have it taken? . . .

have a photo taken

2 ROLE PLAY *A friend in need*

Student A: Choose one of these problems. Decide on the details of the problem. Then tell your partner about it and get some advice.

I'm looking forward to my vacation, but I haven't saved enough money.
I don't get along with my . . . . We're always fighting.
I can't take care of my pet anymore. I don't know what to do.

Student B: Your partner is telling you about a problem. Ask questions about the problem. Then consider the situation and offer two pieces of advice.

Change roles and choose another situation.

useful expressions
Have you thought about . . . ?
It might be a good idea to . . .
Maybe you could . . .
Why don't you . . . ?

3 LISTENING *How good is your history?*

A Listen to people discuss the questions. Write the correct answers.

1. When was the first Iditarod? ....
2. How long did apartheid exist in South Africa? ....
3. When did a spacecraft first land on Mars? ....
4. How long was the Berlin Wall up? ....
5. How long has the modern Olympics existed? ....

B *Group work* Write three more questions about achievements, disasters, or discoveries. (Make sure you know the answers.) Then take turns asking your questions. Who has the most correct answers?

4 SURVEY *Five years from now . . .*

A *Class activity* How many of your classmates will have done these things in the next five years? Write down the number of "yes" and "no" answers. When someone answers "yes," ask follow-up questions.

	"Yes" answers	"No" answers
1. move to a new city	....	....
2. get a new job	....	....
3. have a(nother) child	....	....
4. travel abroad	....	....
5. change your appearance	....	....
6. get a college or master's degree	....	....

A: Five years from now, will you have moved to a new city?
B: Yes, I think I will have moved away from here.
A: Where do you think you'll move to?
B: I'd like to live in Shanghai.
A: Really? What will you be doing there? . . .

B *Group work* Tally the results of the survey as a group. Then take turns telling the class any additional information you found out.

Shanghai

"Very few people think they will have moved to a new city in five years. Only two people think that they will move. One person thinks he'll move to Shanghai, and one person thinks she'll move to Boston."

WHAT'S NEXT?

Look at your Self-assessment again. Do you need to review anything?

 Life's little lessons

1 SNAPSHOT

RITES OF PASSAGE — Some important life events

- First birthday
  (or first 100 days, as in Korea)
- First haircut/losing your first tooth
- First day of school
- Confirmation or bar/bat mitzvah
- Sweet 16
  (or Sweet 15, as in Latin America)
- First job
- High school graduation
- 20th birthday
  (or 21st birthday, as in the United States and Canada)
- Marriage
- Becoming a parent

Source: *Peace Corps Handbook for RPCV Speakers*

Which of these rites of passage, or life events, are important in your country? Check (✓) the events.
What are three other rites of passage for people in your country?
Have any of these things recently happened to you or someone you know?

2 CONVERSATION *I was really immature.*

A ▶ Listen and practice.

Alan: So what were you like when you were younger?
Carol: When I was a kid, I was kind of irresponsible.
Alan: You? Really? What made you change?
Carol: Graduating from high school.
Alan: What do you mean?
Carol: Well, until I graduated, I'd never had any important responsibilities. But then, I went off to college. . . .
Alan: I know what you mean. I was really immature when I was a teenager.
Carol: So what made *you* change?
Alan: I think I became more mature after I got my first job and moved away from home. Once I had a job, I became totally independent.
Carol: Where did you work?
Alan: I worked for my dad at the bank.

B ▶ Listen to the rest of the conversation.
What was another turning point for Carol? for Alan?

3 GRAMMAR FOCUS

A Match the clauses in column A with appropriate information in column B.
(More than one answer is possible.) Then compare with a partner.

A

1. By the time I was 15, ...
2. Until I started working part time, ...
3. The moment I got my first paycheck, ...
4. As soon as I left home, ...
5. Once I started sharing an apartment, ...
6. After I began a relationship, ...
7. Before I traveled abroad, ...
8. Until I got really sick, ...

B

a. I didn't appreciate my own country.
b. I began to understand the value of money.
c. I learned how to communicate better.
d. I realized that I wasn't a child anymore.
e. I had learned how to take care of myself.
f. I learned how to get along better with people.
g. I had never saved any money.
h. I hadn't understood the importance of good health.

B Which of the clauses in column A can you relate to your life?
Add your own information to those clauses. Then compare with a partner.

C *Group work* What do you think people learn from these events? Write sentences
using time clauses in the present. Then take turns reading and talking about them.

1. you get your driver's license
2. you go out on your first date
3. you get your first job
4. you get a credit card
5. you buy your first bike, moped, or car
6. you have your own bank account
7. you get married
8. you become a parent

> 1. *After you get your driver's license, you find out that all your friends want rides.*

4 LISTENING Important events

A ▶ Listen to three people describe important events in their lives. Complete the chart.

	Event	How it affected him or her
1. Sally	....	....
2. Henry	....	....
3. Debbie	....	....

B ▶ Listen again. What do these three people have in common?

5 SPEAKING Milestones

A *Pair work* In your country, how old are people when these things happen?

go to school for the first time   get married
get a driver's license   become a parent
move out of the parents' home   retire

B *Group work* Think of two ways in which each event in part A is important. What do you think life is like before and after each event? Join another pair and discuss.

"Before I went to school, I was quiet and shy. Once I started going to school, I realized how exciting it was to be around so many other children!"

6 WORD POWER Behavior and personality

A *Pair work* At what age do you think people tend to behave in these ways? Check (✓) one or more ages for each behavior.

	In their teens	In their 20s	In their 30s	In their 40s	In their 60s
ambitious	☐	☐	☐	☐	☐
argumentative	☐	☐	☐	☐	☐
carefree	☐	☐	☐	☐	☐
conscientious	☐	☐	☐	☐	☐
naive	☐	☐	☐	☐	☐
pragmatic	☐	☐	☐	☐	☐
rebellious	☐	☐	☐	☐	☐
sensible	☐	☐	☐	☐	☐
sophisticated	☐	☐	☐	☐	☐

B *Group work* Take turns using words in part A to describe people you know.

PERSPECTIVES *I should've . . .*

A ▶ Listen to Maya Misery talk about her regrets.

"If I'd listened to my mother, I would have learned to play a musical instrument."

"I should have studied something more practical when I was in college."

"If I hadn't been so irresponsible, I could have made better grades."

"If I'd been more ambitious in college, I could have learned to speak another language."

"I shouldn't have waited so long to choose a major."

"If I hadn't wasted so much money last year, I would have my own apartment now."

B Do you have any similar regrets? What do you suggest to help Maya feel better?

8 **GRAMMAR FOCUS**

> **Expressing regret and describing hypothetical situations** ▶
>
> I **should have studied** something more practical when I was in college.
> I **shouldn't have waited** so long to choose a major.
>
> *Describing hypothetical situations*
> **If I'd been** more ambitious in college, I **could have learned** another language.
> **If I hadn't wasted** so much money last year, I **would have** my own apartment now.

A For each statement, write a sentence expressing regret. Then talk with a partner about which statements are true for you.

1. I was very rebellious when I was younger.
2. I didn't pay attention to what I ate as a kid.
3. I didn't make a lot of friends when I was in high school.
4. I was very argumentative when I was a teenager.
5. I was too naive when I started looking for my first job.

> 1. I should have been more
> conscientious when I
> was younger.

B Match the clauses in column A with appropriate information in column B.

A

1. If I'd listened to my parents, ...
2. If I'd been more active, ...
3. If I'd been more ambitious, ...
4. If I'd studied harder in school, ...
5. If I'd saved my money, ...

B

a. I wouldn't be as broke as I am now.
b. I could have learned a lot more.
c. I would have made more pragmatic decisions.
d. I wouldn't be overweight.
e. I could have gotten a promotion.

C Add your own information to the clauses in column A. Then compare in groups.

9 INTERCHANGE 11 *If things were different...*

Imagine if things were different. Go to Interchange 11.

10 PRONUNCIATION *Reduction of* have *and* been

A ▶ Listen and practice. Notice how **have** and **been** are reduced in these sentences.

I should ~~have been~~ less selfish when I was younger.
If I'd ~~been~~ more ambitious, I could ~~have~~ gotten a promotion.

B *Pair work* Complete these sentences and practice them. Pay attention to the reduced forms of **have** and **been**.

I should have been . . . when I was younger.   If I'd been more . . . , I could have . . .
I should have been . . . in high school.   If I'd been less . . . , I would have . . .

11 LISTENING *Regrets*

A ▶ Listen to people describe their regrets. Complete the chart.

	What does he or she regret?	Why does he or she regret it?
1. Barbara		
2. Alex		
3. Yi-shun		

B ▶ Listen again. What effect have the regrets had on each person's life?

12 WRITING *A letter of apology*

A Think about something you regret doing that you want to apologize for. Consider the questions below. Then write a letter of apology.

What did you do? What were the consequences?
Is there any way you can undo those consequences?

> *Dear Jonathan,*
>   *I'm so sorry you worked so hard making all those cookies for my party! I should've told you that the party was canceled, but I got really busy at work and didn't get around to calling everybody. If I'd been more conscientious . . .*

B *Pair work* Read your partner's letter. Talk about what you would have done if you'd had a similar regret.

13 READING

If You Could Do It All Again

Skim the article. Who wanted to be a teacher? Who wants to be a musician? Who wants to go to college?

Laura

Evan

Kelly

After I finished high school, I just wasn't ready to go on to college. I really needed some time to figure out what I wanted to do. I had saved up a lot of money, so I used it to travel through Eastern Europe for six months. It was an amazing experience, and I learned a lot about myself. Once I got home, I was ready to start college. Now the only trouble is that I don't have enough money to pay for it! Before I decided to take such an expensive trip, I should have thought more pragmatically about my financial decisions.

By the time I was 22, I was the head of the public relations department in a major telecommunications company. Now I'm a vice president. I love the excitement, the status, the security, and the money. But sometimes I wake up in the middle of the night and wonder, "What am I doing? Who am I?" When I was growing up, I always thought I would become a teacher or maybe an artist. Sometimes it seems like I have everything, and yet I have nothing.

I started playing the violin when I was only five. By the time I was in high school, I knew I wanted to be a musician. Then last spring, I was chosen to participate in a summer music program in London! This was a huge honor that I wasn't expecting. Unfortunately, my brother's wedding was also planned for the summer. Of course, I couldn't miss the wedding, so I had to say "no" to London. Now I sort of resent that I couldn't go. Sometimes I think that if I'd been a little more selfish, I could have done both.

A Read the article. Then check (✓) the correct boxes to answer these questions.

	Laura	Evan	Kelly
1. Whose success could be described as . . . ?			
a. a financial success	☐	☐	☐
b. the courage to explore new things	☐	☐	☐
c. a commitment to family	☐	☐	☐
2. Whose regrets could be described as . . . ?			
a. a missed opportunity	☐	☐	☐
b. losing oneself to achieve success	☐	☐	☐
c. being shortsighted	☐	☐	☐
3. Whose problem could be described as . . . ?			
a. a financial problem	☐	☐	☐
b. feeling cheated	☐	☐	☐
c. feeling confused	☐	☐	☐

B *Group work* Which of the three people seems the happiest? the least happy? Do you have any regrets about things in your past? What would you do differently?

12 The right stuff

SNAPSHOT

$uccess $tories	Five of the world's most successful businesses	
	Main products	**Fact**
Coca-Cola	soft drinks, juice, and bottled water	*Coca-Cola* is the best known English word in the world after *OK*.
Sony	electronics equipment, movies, and TV	Some early products included radio adapters and rice cookers.
Levi Strauss	jeans and casual clothing	The first jeans were made for men looking for gold in California.
Nike	athletic shoes and sports clothing	Nike is named for the Greek goddess of victory.
Nestlé	chocolate, instant coffee, and bottled water	Nestlé means *little nest*, which symbolizes security and family.

Source: *Hoover's Handbook of American Business 2003*; www.sony.net; www.nestle.dk

Which of these products exist in your country? Are they successful?
Can you think of three successful companies in your country? What do they produce?

PERSPECTIVES

A ▶ A new shopping and entertainment complex is conducting a survey. Listen to the survey. Number the choices from 1 to 3.

What makes a business successful?

1 Most important
2 Somewhat important
3 Least important

1. **In order for a shopping mall to succeed, it has to have**
   ☐ a variety of stores   ☐ a convenient location   ☐ sufficient parking
2. **To run a popular Internet café, it's a good idea to have**
   ☐ plenty of computers   ☐ good snacks and drinks   ☐ late opening hours
3. **In order to operate a successful cinema, you need to make sure it has**
   ☐ the latest movies   ☐ good snacks and drinks   ☐ big screens
4. **To establish a trendy restaurant, it's important to have**
   ☐ fashionable servers   ☐ delicious food   ☐ good music
5. **For an athletic center to be profitable, it needs to have**
   ☐ good trainers   ☐ modern exercise equipment   ☐ a variety of classes
6. **For a concert hall to be successful, it should have**
   ☐ excellent acoustics   ☐ comfortable seats   ☐ affordable tickets

B *Group work* Compare your answers in groups. Do you agree on the most important success factors?

3 PRONUNCIATION Reduced words

A ▶ Listen and practice. Notice how certain words a▮ ▮luced in conversation.

In order **før ȧ** café **tø** succeed, it needs **tø** have good food **ånd** service.
Før ȧn airline **tø** be successful, it has **tø** maintain ȧ good safety record.

B *Pair work* Take turns reading the sentences in Exercise 2 aloud. Use your
first choice to complete each sentence. Pay attention to reduced words.

4 GRAMMAR FOCUS

> ### Describing purpose ▶
>
> *Infinitive clauses*
>
> | | |
> |---|---|
> | **To run** a popular Internet café, | it's a good idea to have late opening hours. |
> | **(In order) to establish** a trendy restaurant, | it's important to have fashionable servers. |
>
> *Infinitive clauses with for*
>
> | | |
> |---|---|
> | **For** an athletic center **to be** profitable, | it needs to have modern exercise equipment. |
> | **(In order) for** a shopping mall **to succeed**, | it has to have a convenient location. |

A Match each goal with a suggestion. (More than one answer is possible.)
Then practice the sentences with a partner. Pay attention to the reduced words.

Goals

1. For a health club to attract new people, ...
2. In order to run a profitable restaurant, ...
3. To establish a successful new dance club, ...
4. For a coffee bar to succeed, ...
5. In order for a magazine to succeed, ...
6. To run a successful clothing boutique, ...

Suggestions

a. you need to hire a talented chef.
b. it's a good idea to offer desserts, too.
c. you need to keep up with the latest styles.
d. it needs to have great music and lighting.
e. it has to offer the latest types of equipment.
f. it has to provide useful information.

B *Pair work* Think of two more suggestions
for each of the goals in part A.

C *Group work* Look at the picture of
a coffee shop. For it to stay popular,
what five things should be done?

A: For this coffee shop to stay popular,
   I think it needs a new manager.
B: And in order to keep customers,
   it's important to . . .

5 WORD POWER Qualities for success

A *Pair work* What qualities are important for success? Add one more adjective to each list. Then rank them from 1 to 6.

A model

- ☐ fashionable
- ☐ gorgeous
- ☐ industrious
- ☐ muscular
- ☐ slender
- ☐ ....

A salesperson

- ☐ clever
- ☐ charming
- ☐ knowledgeable
- ☐ persuasive
- ☐ tough
- ☐ ....

A magazine

- ☐ affordable
- ☐ attractive
- ☐ entertaining
- ☐ informative
- ☐ well written
- ☐ ....

B *Group work* Describe the qualities you feel are most important.

"For a model to be successful, he or she needs to be . . ."

6 ROLE PLAY You're hired!

Student A: Interview two people for one of these jobs. What qualities do they need for success? Decide who is more qualified for the job.

Students B and C: You are applying for the same job. What are your best qualities? Convince the interviewer that you are more qualified for the job.

host for a political talk show   server at a trendy café   exercise equipment salesperson

A: To be a good host for a political talk show, you need to be knowledgeable.
B: Well, I follow politics closely, and I'm also tough. I'm not afraid to ask hard questions.
C: I'm fascinated by politics, and I'm industrious, so I would do thorough research.

7 CONVERSATION It's the newest "in" place.

A ▶ Listen and practice.

Mayumi: What's your favorite club, Ben?
Ben: The Soul Club. They have fabulous music, and it's never crowded, so it's easy to get in.
Mayumi: That's funny. There's always a long wait outside my favorite club. I like it because it's always packed.
Ben: Why do you think it's so popular?
Mayumi: Well, it just opened a few months ago, everything is brand new and modern, and lots of fashionable people go there. It's called The Casablanca.
Ben: Oh, right! It's the newest "in" place. I hear the reason people go there is just to be seen.
Mayumi: Exactly! Do you want to go some night?
Ben: I thought you'd never ask!

B *Class activity* What are the "in" places in your city? Do you ever go to any of these places? Why or why not?

8 GRAMMAR FOCUS

Giving reasons ▶

I like The Casablanca **because** it's always packed.
Since it's always so packed, there's a long wait outside the club.
It's popular **because of** the fashionable people.
The Soul Club is famous **for** its fabulous music.
Due to the crowds, The Casablanca is difficult to get in to.
The reason (that/why) people go there **is** just to be seen.

A Complete the paragraph with *because, since, because of, for, due to,* and *the reason*. Then compare with a partner.

MTV is one of the most popular television networks in the world. People love MTV not only .... its music videos, but also .... its clever and diverse programming. .... it keeps its shows up-to-the-minute, young people watch MTV for the latest fads in music and fashion. MTV is also well known .... its music awards show. .... so many people watch it is to see all the fashionable guests. MTV even has shows about politics. These shows are popular .... they are informative and appealing to young people. .... MTV's widespread popularity, many teenagers have become less industrious with their homework!

B What reason explains the success of each situation? (More than one answer is possible.) Compare ideas with a partner.

Situation

1. Family-owned shops are closing ....
2. People love Levi's jeans ....
3. The BBC is well known ....
4. Huge supermarket chains are popular ....
5. People everywhere drink Coca-Cola ....
6. Teenagers watch MTV ....
7. Nike is a popular brand of clothing ....
8. Many people like megastores ....

Reason

a. since prices are generally more affordable.
b. due to an excess of shopping malls.
c. because they have always been fashionable.
d. for its attractive and charming hosts.
e. because of its informative programming.
f. for their big choice of products.
g. since it advertises worldwide.
h. because the advertising is clever and entertaining.

C *Pair work* Suggest two more reasons for each success in part B.

"I think family-owned shops are closing because megastores have cheaper prices."

9 INTERCHANGE 12 Entrepreneurs

How effective is advertising? Go to Interchange 12.

10 LISTENING Radio commercials

▶ Listen to three radio commercials advertising businesses. What are two special features of each place? What slogan does each place use?

	Features	Slogan
1. Maggie's	....	....
	....	....
2. Sports Pro	....	....
	....	....
3. Mexi-Grill	....	....
	....	....

11 SPEAKING Catchy slogans

A *Pair work* Look at these slogans. What products do you think they are advertising? Match each slogan with a product in the box.

It's the Real Thing.

"All the News That's Fit to Print"

The happiest place on Earth.

JUST DO IT.

GOOD TO THE LAST DROP

Bet you can't eat just one.

coffee
a daily newspaper
potato chips
a soft drink
an amusement park
sports clothing

A: "It's the real thing" might be used to advertise . . .
B: But it also could be from an ad for . . .
C: I think it's used in . . . ads.

B *Class activity* What other famous slogans can you think of?

12 WRITING A TV commercial

A Choose one of your favorite products. Read the questions and make notes about the best way to sell it. Then write a one-minute TV commercial.

What's good or unique about the product?
Why would someone want to buy or use it?
Can you think of a clever name or slogan?

B *Group work* Take turns presenting your commercials. What is good about each one? Can you give any suggestions to improve them?

> Are you looking for a high-quality
> TV that is also attractively designed?
> Buy a Star TV. Star is the most
> popular name in electronics because
> of its commitment to excellence and . . .

The Wrong Stuff

Look at the picture and the first sentence of the article. Why is market research important to companies that want to sell their products internationally?

If a business wants to sell its products internationally, it had better do some market research first. This is a lesson that some large American corporations have learned the hard way.

What's in a name?
Sometimes the problem is the name. When General Motors introduced its Chevy Nova into Latin America, it overlooked the fact that *No va* in Spanish means "It doesn't go." Sure enough, the Chevy Nova never went anywhere in Latin America.

Translation problems
Sometimes it's the slogan that doesn't work. No company knows this better than Pepsi-Cola, with its "Come alive with Pepsi!" campaign. The campaign was so successful in the United States, Pepsi translated its slogan literally for its international campaign. As it turned out, the translations weren't quite right. Pepsi was pleading with Germans to "Come out of the grave" and telling the Chinese that "Pepsi brings your ancestors back from the grave."

A picture's worth a thousand words
Other times, the problem involves packaging. A picture of a smiling, round-cheeked baby has helped sell countless jars of Gerber baby food. So when Gerber marketed its products in Africa, it kept the picture on the jar. What Gerber didn't realize was that in many African countries, the picture on the jar shows what the jar has in it.

Twist of fate
Even cultural and religious factors – and pure coincidence – can be involved. Thom McAn shoes have a Thom McAn "signature" inside. To people in Bangladesh, this signature looked like Arabic script for the word Allah. In that country, feet are considered unclean, and Muslims felt the company was insulting God's name by having people walk on it.

A Read the article. Then for each statement, check (✓) True, False, or Not given.

	True	False	Not given
1. General Motors did extensive research before introducing the Chevy Nova.	☐	☐	☐
2. The "Come alive with Pepsi!" campaign worked well in the United States.	☐	☐	☐
3. Pepsi still sold well in Germany and China.	☐	☐	☐
4. Gerber changed its packaging after the problem in Africa.	☐	☐	☐
5. Thom McAn used the Arabic script for the word Allah in their shoes.	☐	☐	☐
6. The problem for Thom McAn was the company's name.	☐	☐	☐

B Look at the marketing problems below. In each situation, was the problem the result of name (**N**) or translation (**T**)?

.... 1. The Ford Fiera didn't sell well in Spain, where *fiera* means "ugly old woman."

.... 2. Braniff Airline's "Fly in leather" slogan was meant to promote its comfortable new seats. In Spanish, the company was telling passengers to "Fly with no clothes on."

C *Group work* Think of two products from your country: one that would sell well around the world, and one that might not sell as well. Why would one sell well, but not the other? What changes could help the second product sell better?

Units 11-12 Progress check

SELF-ASSESSMENT

How well can you do these things? Check (✓) the boxes.

I can	Very well	OK	A little
Describe important events with time clauses (Ex. 1)	▢	▢	▢
Talk about behavior and personality (Ex. 2)	▢	▢	▢
Express regrets about the past using past modals (Ex. 2)	▢	▢	▢
Describe hypothetical situations using *if* clauses (Ex. 2)	▢	▢	▢
Listen to, understand, and give reasons for success (Ex. 3, 4)	▢	▢	▢
Describe purpose with infinitive clauses and clauses with *for* (Ex. 4)	▢	▢	▢

1 SPEAKING *Lessons to live by*

A What are two important events for each of these age groups? Complete the chart.

Children	Teenagers	People in their 20s	People in their 40s
....	....	....	....
....	....	....	....

B *Group work* Talk about the events. Why is each event important? What do people learn from each event?

A: Starting school is an important event for children.
B: What do children learn from starting school?
A: Once they start school, . . .

useful expressions	
after	once
as soon as	before
the moment	until
by the time	

2 GAME *A chain of events*

A Write three regrets you have about the past.

B *Group work* What if the situations were different? Take turns. One student expresses a regret. The next student adds a hypothetical result, and so on, for as long as you can.

A: I should have been more ambitious during college.
B: If I'd been more ambitious, I would have gone abroad.
C: If I'd gone abroad, I could have . . .

我的名字是Lauren。

84

3 LISTENING *Success story*

A ⊙ Listen to a business consultant discuss the factors necessary for a restaurant to be successful. Check (✓) the ones she says are important.

☐ advertising ☐ concept ☐ decor ☐ food ☐ name ☐ location

B ⊙ Listen again. In your own words, write the reason why each factor is important.

Factor	Why is it important?
1.	....
2.	....
3.	....

4 DISCUSSION *The secrets of success*

A *Pair work* Choose two businesses and discuss what they need to be successful. Then write three sentences describing the most important factors.

☐ a high-rise hotel ☐ a language school ☐ a music store
☐ an Internet bookstore ☐ a gourmet supermarket ☐ an online banking service

> *In order for a hotel to be successful, it has to be affordable.*

the Waldorf-Astoria

B *Group work* Join another pair. Share your ideas. Do they agree?

A: We think in order for a hotel to be successful, it has to be affordable.
B: Really? We think some of the most successful hotels are very expensive.

C *Group work* Now choose a popular business that you know about. What are the reasons for its success?

"I think the Waldorf-Astoria hotel is successful because the decor is so beautiful."

useful expressions
It's successful because (of) . . .   It's become popular since . . .
It's popular due to . . .   It's famous for . . .
The reason it's successful is . . .

WHAT'S NEXT?

Look at your Self-assessment again. Do you need to review anything?

13 That's a possibility.

Pet Peeves
Common mysteries among friends and acquaintances

Why is it that some people . . . ?

- are always late
- never return phone calls or answer e-mails
- don't listen carefully when you talk to them
- act differently in front of people they want to impress
- always look messy
- never remember to return things
- are always short of money
- never know when to go home or get off the phone

Source: Interviews with people between the ages of 16 and 45

Which of the above pet peeves do you have about people you know? Which one is the worst?
Underline a pet peeve you could be accused of. When and why are you guilty of it?
What other things do you get peeved about?

2 **CONVERSATION** *What happened?*

A ▶ Listen and practice.

Jackie: You asked Beth to be here around 7:00, didn't you?
  Bill: Yes. What time is it now?
Jackie: It's almost 8:00. I wonder what happened.
  Bill: Hmm. She might have forgotten the time. Why don't I call and see if she's on her way?

A few minutes later

  Bill: I got her voice mail, so she must not have turned on her cell phone.
Jackie: I hope she didn't have a problem on the road. Her car could have broken down or something.
  Bill: Of course she may have simply forgotten and done something else today.
Jackie: No, she couldn't have forgotten – I just talked to her about it yesterday. I guess we should start without her.

B ▶ Listen to the rest of the conversation. What happened?

3 PRONUNCIATION Reduction in past modals

A Listen and practice. Notice how **have** is reduced in these sentences.

He must ~~have~~ forgotten the date.   She might ~~have~~ had a problem on the road.

B Listen and practice. Notice that **not** is not contracted or reduced in these sentences.

He may **not** have remembered it.   She must **not** have caught her bus.

4 GRAMMAR FOCUS

Past modals for degrees of certainty

It's almost certain.
She **must have left** already.
She **must not have turned on** her cell phone.

It's not possible.
She **couldn't have been** at home.

It's possible.
She **may/might have forgotten** the time.
She **may/might not have remembered** the time.
Her car **could have broken down.**

A Read each situation and choose the best explanation. Then practice with a partner. (Pay attention to the reduced forms in past modals.)

Situation

1. Jane is in a terrible mood today. ....
2. Brian got a call and looked worried. ....
3. The teacher looks very happy today. ....
4. Maura couldn't keep her eyes open. ....
5. Jeff was fired from his job. ....
6. My cousin is short of money again. ....

Explanation

a. He may have gotten a raise.
b. She must not have gotten enough sleep.
c. He might not have done his work on time.
d. She could have had a fight with her boyfrien
e. She must have spent too much last month.
f. He couldn't have heard good news.

B *Pair work* Suggest different explanations for each situation in part A.

5 LISTENING Jumping to conclusions

A *Group work* What do you think happened? Offer an explanation for each event.

B Listen to the explanations for the two events in part A and take notes.
What *did* happen? How similar were your explanations?

6 SPEAKING What's your explanation?

A *Pair work* What do you think were the reasons for these events? Suggest two different explanations for each.

1. Two people were having dinner in a restaurant. One suddenly got up and ran out of the restaurant.
2. A woman living alone returned home and found the TV and radio turned on. They weren't on when she went out.
3. Two friends met again after not seeing each other for many years. One looked at the other and burst out laughing.

B *Group work* Each student thinks of two situations like the ones in part A. Others suggest explanations.

A: Late one night, a man wearing pajamas was seen in a field. He was carrying a broken leash.
B: Well, he might have been sleepwalking and . . .

7 INTERCHANGE 13 Photo plays

What's your best explanation for some unusual events? Go to Interchange 13.

8 PERSPECTIVES She's driving me crazy!

A Listen to three friends talking to one another on the phone. Check (✓) the response you think is best for each person's problem.

B Do you talk about pet peeves with your friends? Do they give you advice?

9 GRAMMAR FOCUS

Past modals for opinions and advice ◐

Giving opinions

You **should have called** her on the phone.
She **shouldn't have kept** your notes this long.

Giving advice

You **could have been** more understanding.
I **would have borrowed** someone else's notes.
I **wouldn't have lent** them to her.

A Complete the conversations using past modals with the verbs given. Then practice with a partner.

1. A: I invited my boyfriend over to meet my parents, but he arrived wearing torn jeans. He looked so messy!
   B: Well, he .... (dress) neatly. I .... (ask) him to wear something nicer.

2. A: John borrowed my car and dented it. When he returned it, he didn't even say anything about it!
   B: He .... (tell) you! Well, I .... (not lend) it to him in the first place. He's a terrible driver.

3. A: I'm exhausted. Mary came over and stayed until 2 A.M.!
   B: She .... (not stay) so late. You .... (start) yawning. Maybe she would have gotten the hint!

4. A: Tom invited me to a play, but I ended up paying for us both!
   B: I .... (not pay) for him. He .... (not invite) you if he was short of money.

B *Pair work* Think of another suggestion or comment for each situation above.

10 WORD POWER Reactions

A Megan's boyfriend forgot her birthday. How does she react?
Match each reaction with the best example.

Reaction

1. an assumption ....
2. a criticism ....
3. a demand ....
4. an excuse ....
5. a prediction ....
6. a suggestion ....
7. a suspicion ....
8. a warning ....

Example

a. If you do it again, you'll have to find a new girlfriend.
b. I bet you were out with another woman!
c. You can be so inconsiderate.
d. You'll probably forget our anniversary, too!
e. Now you have to take me out to dinner . . . twice.
f. You must have wanted to break up with me.
g. You know, you ought to buy me flowers.
h. It's OK, you must feel really sorry!

B *Group work* Imagine that someone was late for class, or choose another situation. Give an example of each reaction in the list above.

11 LISTENING *What should they have done?*

A ▶ Listen to descriptions of three situations. What would have been the best thing to do in each situation? Check (✓) the best suggestion.

1. ☐ Dennis should have called a locksmith.
   ☐ He should have called a tow truck.
   ☐ He did the right thing.

2. ☐ Diana should have turned up her radio to keep out the noise.
   ☐ She should have called the neighbors to see what was happening.
   ☐ She did the right thing.

3. ☐ Simon should have taken the ring and put an ad in the newspaper.
   ☐ He should have taken the ring and called the police when he got home.
   ☐ He did the right thing.

B *Pair work* What would you have done in each situation in part A?

12 DISCUSSION *You could have . . .*

A *Pair work* Work together to think of three interesting predicaments.

"We were at a friend's house for dinner last night. He had cooked all day, but the food was awful! We didn't want to hurt his feelings."

B *Group work* Pairs take turns stating their predicaments. Others say what the pair could, should, or might have done.

A: You should have told him you weren't feeling well.
B: Or you could have eaten it really slowly. . . .

13 WRITING *About a predicament*

A Think of a predicament from your own experience. Write a paragraph describing the situation, but don't explain how you resolved it.

> My teacher invited my class to a party and told us to "dress up." The problem was, the party just happened to be on Halloween night, and I thought "dress up" meant to wear a costume! I arrived at the party dressed as a bee, and everyone else was wearing nice clothes! I was so embarrassed.

B *Pair work* Exchange papers. Write a short paragraph giving advice for your partner's predicament.

C Read the advice for your predicament. Tell your partner how you resolved it. Whose solution was better?

The Blue Lights of Silver Cliff

Look at the picture. What do you think the "blue lights" are?

oday, the town of Silver Cliff, Colorado, has a population of only 100 people. Once, however, it was a prosperous mining town where thousands came with dreams of finding silver and making their fortune.

Late one night in 1880, a group of miners were headed back to their camp after a good time in town. They were still laughing and joking as they approached the graveyard on a hill outside Silver Cliff. Then one of the men yelled and pointed toward the graveyard. The others fell silent. On top of each grave, they saw flamelike blue lights. These eerie lights seemed to be dancing on the graves, disappearing and then appearing again.

This was the first sighting of the blue lights of Silver Cliff. There have been many other sightings over the years. In 1969, Edward Lineham from *National Geographic* magazine visited the graveyard. Lineham's article tells of his experience: "I saw them. . . . Dim, round spots of blue-white light glowed ethereally among the graves. I . . . stepped forward for a better look. They vanished. I aimed my flashlight at one eerie glow and switched it on. It revealed only a tombstone."

Lineham and others have suggested various explanations for the lights. The lights might have been reflections of lights from the town, but Silver Cliff's lights seemed too dim to have this effect. They could have been caused by radioactive ore, though there's no evidence of radioactivity. They may also have been caused by gases from rotting matter. This usually happens in swamps, however, and the area around Silver Cliff is dry. Or, perhaps the lights are from the helmets of dead miners wandering the hills in search of their fortune.

A Read the article. Then answer these questions.

1. How has Silver Cliff changed over the years?
2. Where were the blue lights first seen?

3. Who saw the blue lights first?
4. What do the blue lights look like?

B Which of these statements are facts? Which are opinions? Check (✓) Fact or Opinion.

	Fact	Opinion
1. Today, the town of Silver Cliff has a population of 100 people.	☐	☐
2. The miners saw flamelike blue lights on top of each grave.	☐	☐
3. Edward Lineham suggested various explanations for the lights.	☐	☐
4. The lights were actually reflections of lights from the town.	☐	☐
5. There was no evidence of radioactivity.	☐	☐
6. The lights were from the helmets of dead miners.	☐	☐

C *Group work* Which of the explanations for the blue lights do you think is the most satisfactory? Why? Can you think of any other possible explanations?

14 Behind the scenes

1 SNAPSHOT

MOVIE FIRSTS

The first . . .

Silent narrative film – *The Great Train Robbery* (1903)

Mickey Mouse cartoon (1928)

Drive-in movie theater (1933)

Color epic – *Gone with the Wind* (1939)

Full-length three-dimensional (3-D) feature film – *House of Wax* (1953)

Movie to gross $100 million – *Jaws* (1975)

IMAX 3-D film – *We are Born of Stars* (1985)

Advanced computer technology – *Terminator 2* (1991)

Computer-animated feature film – *Toy Story* (1995)

Movie to gross over $1 billion – *Titanic* (1998)

Sources: *New York Public Library Book of Chronologies*; IMAX Corporation; SIGGRAPH; www.onlygoodmovies.net; www.pbs.org

Have you ever seen any of these movies? Did you enjoy them?
Have you ever seen a silent film? a Mickey Mouse cartoon? a 3-D film?
  a movie at a drive-in? an IMAX film?
Are there many movies made in your country? Name a few of your favorites.

2 CONVERSATION Movies are hard work!

A ▶ Listen and practice.

Ryan: Working on movies must be really exciting.
Nina: Oh, yeah, but it's also very hard work. A one-minute scene in a film can take days to shoot.
Ryan: Really? Why is that?
Nina: Well, a scene isn't filmed just once. Lots of different shots have to be taken. Only the best ones are used in the final film.
Ryan: So, how many times does a typical scene need to be shot?
Nina: It depends, but sometimes as many as 20 times. One scene may be shot from five or six different angles.
Ryan: Wow! I didn't realize that.
Nina: Why don't you come visit the studio? I can show you how things are done.
Ryan: Great, I'd love to!

B ▶ Listen to the rest of the conversation.
What else makes working on movies difficult?

3 GRAMMAR FOCUS

The passive to describe process ▷

is/are + past participle	**Modal + be + past participle**
A scene **isn't filmed** just once.	One scene **may be shot** from five or six different angles.
Only the best shots **are used**.	Lots of different shots **have to be taken**.

A The sentences below describe how a movie is made. First, complete
the sentences using the passive. Then compare with a partner.

Before filming

- ☐ To complete the script, it has to .... (divide) into scenes,
  and the filming details need to .... (write out).

- ☐ 1 First, an outline of the script has to .... (prepare).

- ☐ Next, actors .... (choose), locations .... (pick),
  and costumes .... (design). Filming can then begin.

- ☐ Then the outline .... (expand) into a script.

- ☐ After the script .... (complete), a director must
  .... (hire).

During and after filming

- ☐ The final film you see on the screen .... (create) by
  the director and editor out of thousands of different shots.

- ☐ Soon after the film has been edited, music ....
  (compose) and sound effects may .... (add).

- ☐ After the filming .... (finish), the different shots can
  then .... (put together) by the editor and director.

- ☐ 6 Once shooting begins, different shots .... (film)
  separately. Scenes may .... (not shoot) in sequence.

B *Pair work* Number the sentences in part A (before
filming: from 1 to 5; during and after filming: from 6 to 9).

4 LISTENING *I love my job!*

A ▷ Listen to an interview with a TV producer. Write down three things a producer does.

Things a producer does	Personality traits
....	....
....	....
....	....

B ▷ Listen again. What are three personality traits a producer should have? Complete
the chart.

5 SPEAKING Step by step

A *Pair work* Put the pictures in order and describe the steps in each process. Use the vocabulary to help you. How many more steps can you think of?

1. A theater performance: *actors, costumes, play, sets, build, design, rehearse, perform*

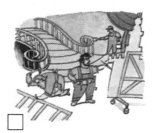   

2. The making of a newspaper: *articles, reporters, research, interviews, print, distribute*

A: Preparing for a theater performance requires many steps.
   First, the script must be written.
B: Right! And after that, the actors are chosen.
C: Then, . . .

B *Pair work* Choose another topic or event: a fashion show, a rock concert, a TV sitcom, or a game. Come up with as many steps as you can think of.

C *Group work* Compare your information from part B with another pair. Are any steps missing?

6 WRITING Describing a process

A Write about one of the topics from Exercise 5 or use your own idea. Describe the different steps in the process.

> Planning a musical is complicated. Before anything else happens, a story must be written. Once the story is written, the rest of the preparations take place. First, music and lyrics need to be composed to accompany the story. Then, a producer must be found. After that, . . .

B *Pair work* Read your partner's paper. Can you think of any more steps?

7 WORD POWER Media professions

A Where do these people work? Complete the chart with the compound nouns.

camera operator	foreign correspondent	movie producer	stunt person
computer programmer	gossip columnist	network installer	support technician
film editor	graphic designer	photo editor	Web-page designer

Film industry	Publishing industry	Computer industry
....	....	....
....	....	....
....	....	....
....	....	....

B *Group work* What exactly do you think each person in part A does?

"A camera operator handles the camera during the filming of a movie."

8 PRONUNCIATION Review of stress in compound nouns

A ▶ The first word in a compound noun usually receives greater stress. Which compound nouns in Exercise 7 do **not** follow this rule? Write the words.

....

B *Pair work* Think of and practice four more compound nouns describing professions.

9 PERSPECTIVES Quiz show

A ▶ Listen to a quiz show. Can you guess the occupations?

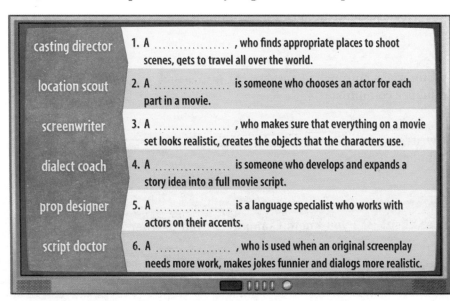

casting director	1. A .... , who finds appropriate places to shoot scenes, gets to travel all over the world.
location scout	2. A .... is someone who chooses an actor for each part in a movie.
screenwriter	3. A .... , who makes sure that everything on a movie set looks realistic, creates the objects that the characters use.
dialect coach	4. A .... is someone who develops and expands a story idea into a full movie script.
prop designer	5. A .... is a language specialist who works with actors on their accents.
script doctor	6. A .... , who is used when an original screenplay needs more work, makes jokes funnier and dialogs more realistic.

B Which of the jobs in part A do you think would be the most interesting? Why? Tell the class.

10

GRAMMAR FOCUS

Defining and non-defining relative clauses ◐

Defining relative clauses are used to identify people.

A dialect coach is a language specialist.   → A dialect coach is a language specialist **who/that**
She works with actors on their accents.   **works with actors on their accents**.

Non-defining relative clauses give further information about people.

A location scout finds places to shoot   → A location scout, **who finds places to**
scenes. He travels all over the world.   **shoot scenes**, travels all over the world.

A Do these sentences contain defining (**D**) or non-defining (**ND**)
clauses? Add commas to the non-defining clauses. Then compare
with a partner.

1. A stunt person is someone who "stands in" for
   an actor during dangerous scenes. ....
2. A special-effects designer who needs advanced
   computer knowledge often spends millions of
   dollars on computer graphics. ....
3. A stagehand is the person who moves the sets
   on stage in a theater production. ....
4. A movie producer who controls the budget
   decides how money will be spent. ....

B Can you add the non-defining relative clauses in
parentheses to the sentences?

1. A foreign correspondent travels all over the world.
   (who writes about events in other countries)

   ....

2. A Web-page designer needs sophisticated computer knowledge.
   (who is a graphic artist)

   ....

3. An editorial page editor gives opinions about current issues.
   (who is a daily newspaper columnist)

   ....

4. A gossip columnist writes about celebrities and scandals.
   (who gets to go to fabulous parties)

   ....

C Write three sentences about jobs you know. Compare with a partner.

a stunt person

INTERCHANGE 14 *Who makes it happen?*

What kinds of people does it take to make a business run? Go to Interchange 14.

Hooray for Bollywood!

Scan the article. Who do you think it was written for?
☐ people who work in the movies ☐ the general public ☐ fans of Bollywood movies

1 A storm forces a plane to make an emergency landing on a deserted island. The only shelter is a spooky house, where a murderer begins killing passengers. So what do these defenseless people do? They have a beach party and perform an elaborate song-and-dance number.

2 This is the world of Bollywood. The scene described above is from the classic Indian film, *Gumnaam*, which was made in the 1960s. It is typical of the kind of movies that are still made in India today.

3 For as long as Hollywood has existed, there has also been an Indian film industry. Because it is based in Bombay (Mumbai), it is popularly called Bollywood – from the words *Bombay* and *Hollywood*. While it is as old as Hollywood, it is much bigger. Bollywood currently has the largest movie industry in the world. It produces more than 1,000 films a year – and as many as 14 million people a day pack into movie theaters to see Bollywood films.

4 While there are many types of films made in India, the most popular are the movies made in Bollywood. The films, which are made in the Hindi language, generally deal with Indian history and social problems. The average Bollywood film runs about three hours, but audiences don't seem to mind the length. The stories are melodramatic: Heroes drive around in flashy cars, actresses twirl around in beautiful costumes, and the poor boy always triumphs against the rich villain. They also feature many musical numbers, usually love songs.

5 Although the films may seem exaggerated to some, that's not how most filmgoers feel. These movies and their stars are beloved by audiences throughout Asia, Africa, and the Middle East. "Every South Asian grows up with some kind of connection to Bollywood," notes Indian writer Suketu Mehta. "In certain ways, it's what unites us."

A Read the article. Find and underline a sentence in the article that answers each question below.

1. How does Bollywood compare to Hollywood?
2. How many Bollywood films are made every year?
3. What language is spoken in Bollywood movies?
4. How long is a typical Bollywood movie?
5. How do audiences feel about the stars of Bollywood movies?

B Find these sentences in the article. Decide whether each sentence is the main idea or a supporting idea in that paragraph. Check (✓) the correct boxes.

	Main idea	Supporting idea
1. This is the world of Bollywood. (par. 2)	☐	☐
2. It produces more than . . . to see Bollywood films. (par. 3)	☐	☐
3. While there are many . . . made in Bollywood. (par. 4)	☐	☐
4. The average Bollywood film . . . mind the length. (par. 4)	☐	☐
5. Although they may sound silly . . . filmgoers feel. (par. 5)	☐	☐

C *Group work* Have you ever seen a Bollywood movie? If so, how did you like it?

Behind the scenes •

Units 13-14 Progress check

SELF-ASSESSMENT

How well can you do these things? Check (✓) the boxes.

I can	Very well	OK	A little
Listen to and express degrees of certainty using past modals (Ex. 1)	▢	▢	▢
Give opinions and advice using past modals (Ex. 2)	▢	▢	▢
React (for example, give a warning) to different situations (Ex. 2)	▢	▢	▢
Use the passive to describe process with *be* and modals (Ex. 3)	▢	▢	▢
Describe people with defining and non-defining relative clauses (Ex. 4)	▢	▢	▢

1 LISTENING *Where did it take place?*

A ◉ Listen to three conversations. Where do you think each conversation takes place? What do you think might have happened? Take notes.

Where the conversation takes place	What might have happened
1.	....
2.	....
3.	....

B *Pair work* Compare your notes. Decide on what happened.

2 DISCUSSION *Tricky situations*

A *Pair work* React to these situations. First, give an opinion or advice using a past modal. Then add another statement using the reaction in parentheses.

1. John was driving too fast and the police stopped him. (a warning)
2. Lisa got an F on her English test. (a criticism)
3. Bill went shopping and spent too much money. (an excuse)
4. Crystal is late to class every morning. (a suggestion)

"John shouldn't have driven so fast. He'd better be careful, or. . . ."

B *Group work* Join another pair and compare your suggestions. Who has the most interesting reaction to each situation?

3 GAME From first to last

A *Group work* Look at these topics. Set a time limit. Talk with your group and write as many steps as you can between the first and last parts of each process.

sending an e-mail

making a cup of tea

First, the computer has to be turned on.

First, some water must be boiled.

....

....

....

....

....

....

....

....

....

....

Finally, the e-mail is delivered to the person's in-box.

Finally, the tea has to be poured from the teapot into the cup.

B *Class activity* Compare your answers. Which group has the most steps?

4 SPEAKING People in your life

A Complete these statements about people in your life.

My mother is a person who ....
My neighbor, who .... , always ....
My good friend is a .... , who ....
My teacher, who .... , is ....
My best friend is someone that ....

B *Pair work* Compare your answers. Ask two follow-up questions about each of your partner's statements.

A: My mother is a person who takes care of everyone's needs before her own.
B: Does she ever get tired of helping everyone but herself?

WHAT'S NEXT?

Look at your Self-assessment again. Do you need to review anything?

15 There should be a law!

IT'S AGAINST THE LAW ...

In the United States	In other countries
• It is against the law to hunt camels in Arizona.	• In Switzerland, it's an offense to hang clothes out to dry on a Sunday.
• In Kentucky, the law requires people to take a bath once a year.	• It is illegal to own a dog – except a Seeing Eye dog – in Iceland.
• In New York City, horses must be given a 15-minute "coffee break" every 2 hours.	• It is against the law not to flush a public toilet in Singapore.
• In the state of Washington, it is illegal to pretend your parents are rich.	• In Finland, people must know how to read in order to get married.

Sources: *It Is Illegal to Quack Like a Duck*; *The Book of Lists*; *www.dumblaws.com*

Which of these laws would you like to have in your city or country? Why?
Can you think of reasons for these laws?
Do you know of any other unusual laws?

2 **PERSPECTIVES**

A ▶ Listen to recommendations people are making at a community meeting.
Do you agree with these proposals for your city? Check (✓) your opinion.

COMMUNITY MEETING NOTES

	strongly agree	somewhat agree	disagree
1. Cyclists should be required to wear a helmet.	☐	☐	☐
2. Pet owners shouldn't be allowed to walk dogs without a leash.	☐	☐	☐
3. People ought to be required to end parties at midnight.	☐	☐	☐
4. Something has got to be done to stop littering.	☐	☐	☐
5. People mustn't be permitted to park motorcycles on the sidewalks.	☐	☐	☐
6. Laws must be passed to control the noise from car alarms.	☐	☐	☐
7. Drivers should only be permitted to honk their horn in case of an emergency.	☐	☐	☐

B In your opinion, what other things should or shouldn't be allowed? Tell the class.

3 GRAMMAR FOCUS

Giving recommendations and opinions ○

When you think something is a good idea
Cyclists **should be required** to wear a helmet.
Pet owners **shouldn't be allowed** to walk dogs without a leash.
People **ought to be required** to end parties at midnight.

When you think something is absolutely necessary
Laws **must be passed** to control the noise from car alarms.
People **mustn't be permitted** to park motorcycles on the sidewalks.
A rule **has to be made** to require cycling lanes on city streets.
Something **has got to be done** to stop littering.

A Complete the sentences positively or negatively. Choose a modal that shows how strongly you feel about these issues.

1. People .... to use cell phones while driving.   (allow)
2. Young people .... to get married before age 15.   (permit)
3. Companies .... to give workers periodic breaks.   (require)
4. People .... to have pets in high-rise apartments.   (allow)
5. Scientists .... to use animals for research.   (permit)
6. Laws .... to ban the sale of handguns.   (pass)
7. The sale of fur products ....   (permit) .
8. Something .... to stop clubs from staying open so late.   (do)

B *Group work* Compare your statements. Do you agree with each other? If not, why not?

A: People shouldn't be allowed to use cell phones while driving. It's dangerous.
B: You may have a point, but laws shouldn't be passed to prevent it. That's too strict.
C: Yes, but in my opinion, . . .

4 DISCUSSION *What's your opinion?*

A *Group work* Think of three reasons *for*, and three reasons *against*, each idea below. Then discuss your views. As a group, form an opinion about each idea.

offering a different opinion

That sounds interesting. But I think . . .
That's not a bad idea. On the other hand, I feel . . .
You may have a point. However, I think . . .

imposing strict dress codes for students
labeling CDs that have offensive lyrics
paying teachers less when their students fail

A: What do you think about imposing strict dress codes for students?
B: I think it's a terrible idea! Students shouldn't be required . . .

B *Class activity* Share your group's opinions and reasons. Who has the most persuasive reasons for and against each position?

There should be a law! • **101**

5 LISTENING *What should be done?*

A ▶ Listen to people discuss problems. What solutions do they suggest?

1. people talking loudly on cell phones in restaurants

2. car alarms going off at night

3. telemarketing salespeople calling too often

Solutions
1. ....
2. ....
3. ....

B *Group work* Do you agree or disagree with the solutions? What do *you* think should be done about each problem?

6 INTERCHANGE 15 *You be the judge!*

What if you could make the rules? Go to Interchange 15.

7 WORD POWER Social issues

A *Pair work* Which of these issues are problems in your community? Check (✓) the appropriate boxes.

- ▢ company downsizing
- ▢ ethnic conflict
- ▢ graffiti
- ▢ gun violence
- ▢ illiteracy
- ▢ inadequate health care
- ▢ lack of affordable child care
- ▢ noise pollution
- ▢ stray animals
- ▢ street crime

a child-care facility

B *Group work* Join another pair of students. Which three problems concern your group the most? What should or can be done about them?

8 CONVERSATION *It isn't cheap, is it?*

A ▶ Listen and practice.

Sarah: Health insurance, child-care bills, rent! Now that I'm going to school and only working part time, I have a hard time making ends meet.

Todd: Health insurance is really expensive, isn't it?

Sarah: Yeah! My company used to pay for it when I was working full time.

Todd: And child care isn't cheap, is it?

Sarah: No, it's not. After I pay for rent and groceries, almost all my money goes to pay for my son's day care.

Todd: Colleges should provide free day care for students with children.

Sarah: I think so, too. But they don't have any services like that at my school.

B ▶ Listen to the rest of the conversation. What is Todd concerned about?

9 GRAMMAR FOCUS

Tag questions for opinions ○

Affirmative statement + negative tag	*Negative statement + affirmative tag*
Health insurance **is** really expensive, **isn't** it?	Child care **isn't** cheap, **is** it?
There **are** lots of criminals in the city, **aren't** there?	There **aren't** enough police, **are** there?
Graffiti **makes** everything look ugly, **doesn't** it?	People **don't care** about our city, **do** they?
Colleges **should** provide day care, **shouldn't** they?	You **can't** find affordable child care, **can** you?

A Add tag questions to these statements. Then compare with a partner.

1. You can't escape advertising nowadays, . . . ?
2. There aren't enough gun-control laws, . . . ?
3. Noise pollution is a major problem here, . . . ?
4. There are more and more homeless people on the streets, . . . ?
5. The sales tax should be lowered, . . . ?
6. It isn't easy to save money these days, . . . ?
7. Downsizing is hurting the economy, . . . ?
8. The city doesn't do enough for stray animals, . . . ?

B What are some things you feel strongly about in your school or city? Write six statements with tag questions.

C *Group work* Take turns reading your statements. Other students respond by giving their opinions.

A: The food in the cafeteria is terrible, isn't it?
B: Yes, it is. They should get a new cook.
C: On the other hand, I like the hamburgers because . . .

10 PRONUNCIATION *Intonation in tag questions*

A ▶ Listen and practice. Use falling intonation in tag questions when you are giving an opinion and want to know if the other person agrees.

Ethnic conflict is a terrible problem, isn't it?   They should make guns illegal, shouldn't they?

B *Pair work* Take turns reading the statements with tag questions from part A of Exercise 9. Give your own opinions when responding.

11 LISTENING *You agree, don't you?*

A ▶ Listen to people give their opinions about current issues in the news. What issues are they talking about?

Issue	Opinions for	Opinions against
1.	....	....
	....	....
2.	....	....
	....	....

B ▶ Listen again. What opinions do you hear? Complete the chart.

C *Group work* What do you think about the issues in part A?

12 WRITING *A letter to a community leader*

A Write a letter to a community leader about a topic in this unit that you feel strongly about. Use these questions to help you.

What is your opinion about the topic or issue?
What are two or three reasons that support your opinion?
What do you think should be done?

> Dear Councilwoman Lopez,
>   I am a student at Morris High School, and I think students ought to be required to wear school uniforms. Students shouldn't be permitted to wear the latest fashions, because this promotes jealousy and competition. Also, students would be able to concentrate on their studies better if . . .

B *Pair work* Exchange letters. Do you agree with your partner's opinion and suggestions? Why or why not?

How Serious Is Plagiarism?

Scan the first paragraph of the article. What does the word *plagiarism* mean?

Recently, a biology teacher in Kansas – a state in the American Midwest – made national, and even international, news. After Christine Pelton discovered that 28 of her 118 students had plagiarized parts of a major project, she gave them failing grades. Although this was the school policy, the students' parents complained. The school board directed Ms. Pelton to change the punishment: They told her that 600 points should be taken from the offenders, rather than the entire 1,800 points. Ms. Pelton resigned in protest.

Why did this become such a significant story? Perhaps it is because so many people feel strongly about what is right and wrong. Although the incident may soon be forgotten, it raised some important questions: What is plagiarism? How serious is it?

The simplest form of plagiarism occurs when someone copies material without giving credit to the source. However, there are also more serious forms, such as when a student pays someone else to write an essay.

Some people claim that copying is necessary to do well in school. They have realized that their own words are not as good as someone else's. Another common argument is that everyone does it, so it's not a big deal. In fact, it has been learned that even some highly respected figures, including Martin Luther King, Jr., have plagiarized.

Although some people find reasons to justify plagiarism, others feel the issue is clear-cut: They feel it is morally wrong, and consider it stealing – a theft of ideas rather than money. These people believe that students who plagiarize benefit unfairly. They receive a better grade than they deserve.

So what about the incident in Kansas? Was the original punishment too severe? Do teachers have the right to tell students and parents what is right or wrong? Ms. Pelton would probably say that the job of a teacher is to do exactly that.

A Read the article. Then number these sentences from 1 (first event) to 6 (last event).

.... a. The teacher's story appeared in national news.
.... b. The teacher gave the students failing grades.
.... c. The students' parents were angry.
.... d. The teacher left her job.
.... e. The group of students cheated on an assignment.
.... f. The school board told the teacher to change the scores.

B Complete the chart.

Arguments to justify plagiarism	Arguments against plagiarism
1.	
2.	

C *Group work* Is it ever OK to copy other people's work? Why or why not?
Do teachers have the right to tell students and parents what is right or wrong?

16 Challenges and accomplishments

1 SNAPSHOT

Three Women Who Made a Difference

"The Saint of the Gutters"

Born: Agnes Gonxha Bojaxhiu in 1910
Died: Mother Teresa in 1997
Major contributions: set up projects around the world to care for poor people, sick people, and children without parents

"Our Fair Lady"

Born: Edda van Heemstra Hepburn-Ruston in 1929
Died: Audrey Hepburn in 1993
Major contributions: as goodwill ambassador for UNICEF, called attention to children's rights and raised money to help them

"The People's Princess"

Born: Lady Diana Spencer in 1961
Died: Diana, Princess of Wales, in 1997
Major contributions: used her fame to focus attention on worldwide problems such as AIDS, drug addiction, and land mines

Source: *People* magazine

Which woman do you think made the biggest difference? Why?
What special qualities do you think these women had in common?
Who are two other people whose lives made a difference? What did they do?

2 PERSPECTIVES Volunteers talk about their work

A ▶ Listen to people talk about their volunteer work. What kind of work do they do? Write the names in the sentences below.

"The most rewarding thing about helping these people is learning from their years of experience."
– Paul

"One of the most difficult aspects of working abroad is being far away from my family."
– Shao-fang

"One of the rewards of working with these people is experiencing their youthful energy and playfulness."
– Mariela

"The most challenging thing about working with these people is determining their different strengths and weaknesses."
– Jack

1. .... teaches in a developing country.
2. .... tutors in an adult literacy program.
3. .... visits senior citizens in a nursing home.
4. .... plays games with children in an orphanage.

B Which kind of volunteer work would you prefer to do? What do you think would be rewarding or challenging about it?

3 GRAMMAR FOCUS

Complex noun phrases containing gerunds ◐

These complex noun phrases contain gerunds. In these
examples, they are also followed by gerunds.

One of the most difficult aspects of working abroad is being far away from my family.
The most rewarding thing about helping them is learning from their years of experience.
One of the rewards of working with them is experiencing their youthful energy.

A *Pair work* Match the questions and responses. Then ask and answer the
questions. Respond using a complex noun phrase followed by a gerund.

Questions

1. What's one of the rewards of being
   a teacher? ....
2. What's one of the most difficult things about
   being an emergency-room nurse? ....
3. What's one of the most challenging things
   about telecommuting from home? ....
4. What's one of the best things about being a
   police officer? ....
5. What's one of the most interesting aspects
   of working abroad? ....
6. What's one of the most difficult aspects of
   doing volunteer work? ....

Responses

a. Dealing with life-or-death situations
   every day.
b. Finding enough time to do it on a
   regular basis.
c. Learning how people in other cultures
   live and think.
d. Helping people learn things that they
   couldn't learn on their own.
e. Getting to know people from all parts
   of society.
f. Not being distracted by household chores
   or hobbies.

A: What's one of the rewards of being a teacher?
B: One of the rewards of being a teacher is helping people learn things
   that they couldn't learn on their own.

B *Group work* Ask the questions in part A again and answer
with your own ideas.

4 PRONUNCIATION *Stress and rhythm*

A ▶ Listen and practice. Notice how stressed words and syllables occur
with a regular rhythm.

The most rewarding thing │ about traveling │ is learning │ about other cultures.

The most frustrating thing │ about working │ in a foreign country │ is missing │ friends and family.

B *Pair work* Take turns reading the sentences in the grammar box in
Exercise 3. Pay attention to stress and rhythm.

5 INTERCHANGE 16 *Viewpoints*

Take a survey about volunteering. Go to Interchange 16.

6 LISTENING *Challenges and rewards*

▶ Listen to these people talk about their work. What is the biggest challenge of each person's job? What is the greatest reward? Complete the chart.

	Biggest challenge	Greatest reward
1. psychologist	....	....
2. camp counselor	....	....
3. firefighter	....	....

7 WORD POWER *Antonyms*

A Find six pairs of opposites in the list. Fill in the blanks. Then compare with a partner.

adaptable   cynical   resourceful   timid
compassionate   dependent   rigid   unimaginative
courageous   insensitive   self-sufficient   upbeat

...... *adaptable* ...... ≠ ...... *rigid* .... ≠ ....

.... ≠ .... ≠ ....

.... ≠ .... ≠ ....

B *Group work* How many words or things can you associate with each word in part A?

A: What words or things do you associate with *adaptable*?
B: Flexible.
C: Easy to get along with.

8 DISCUSSION *A volunteer needs to be . . .*

A *Group work* What are some challenges a volunteer would face for these jobs? Tell the group.

working in a home for the visually impaired
working in a homeless shelter
working in an animal shelter
working in a prison

B *Group work* What characteristics does a volunteer need to meet these challenges?

"The most challenging aspect of working with the visually impaired is coming up with creative descriptions of everything. You'd need to be resourceful."

9 CONVERSATION *I've managed to get good grades. . . .*

A ▶ Listen and practice.

Uncle Ed: Happy birthday, Alison! So how does it feel to be 21?
  Alison: Kind of strange. I suddenly feel a little anxious, like I'm not moving ahead fast enough.
Uncle Ed: But don't you think you've accomplished quite a bit in the last few years?
  Alison: Oh, I've managed to get good grades, but I still haven't been able to decide on a career.
Uncle Ed: Well, what do you hope you'll have achieved by the time you're 30?
  Alison: For one thing, I hope I'll have seen more of the world. But more important than that, I'd like to have made a good start on my career by then.

B *Class activity* How similar are you to Alison? Are you satisfied with your accomplishments so far? What do you want to accomplish next?

10 GRAMMAR FOCUS

Accomplishments and goals ▶

Accomplishments with the present perfect or simple past	Goals with the future perfect or would like to have + past participle
I**'ve managed** to get good grades.	What do you hope you**'ll have achieved**?
(I **managed** to . . .)	I hope I**'ll have seen** more of the world.
I**'ve been able** to accomplish a lot in college.	I**'d like to have made** a good start on my career.
(I **was able** to . . .)	

A What are some of your accomplishments from the last five years? Check (✓) the statements that are true for you. Then think of four more statements about yourself.

- ☐ 1. I've met the person who's right for me.
- ☐ 2. I've learned some important life skills.
- ☐ 3. I was able to complete my degree.
- ☐ 4. I've made an important career move.

B What are some goals you would like to have accomplished in the future? Complete the sentences.

1. One goal I'd like to have reached by next year is . . .
2. In the next three years, I hope I'll have . . .
3. In ten years, I'd like to have . . .
4. By the time I'm 60, I'd like to have . . .

C *Group work* Compare your sentences in parts A and B. What accomplishments do you have in common? What goals?

11 LISTENING Future plans

A ▶ Listen to three young people discuss their plans for the future. What do they hope they'll have achieved by the time they are 30?

1. Justin	2. Jenna	3. Rachel
....	....	....
....	....	....
....	....	....

B *Pair work* Who do you think has the most realistic expectations?

12 WRITING A personal statement for an application

A Imagine you are applying to a school or a job that requires a personal statement. Use these questions to organize your ideas. Make notes and then write a draft.

1. What has your greatest accomplishment been? Has it changed you in any way? How?

2. What are some interesting or unusual facts about yourself that make you a good choice for the job or school?

3. What is something you hope to have achieved in the future? When, why, and how will you reach this goal? Will achieving it change you? Why or why not?

> *I think my greatest accomplishment has been finally getting my diploma at age 30. I've been able to achieve many things in school with the support of my family, and . . .*
> *There are two things I'd really like to have achieved by the time I'm 40. First, I hope I'll have done some traveling. . . .*

B *Group work* Share your statements and discuss each person's accomplishments and goals. Who has the most unusual accomplishment or goal? the most realistic? the most ambitious?

EADING

Young and Gifted

the article. Who is a newcomer to their sport?
is trilingual? Who is a college student?

osé Cruz's South Texas community is 99 percent Hispanic. Although their
ependence on Spanish could be seen as something that makes life in America
nore difficult, José and his high school classmates found a way of turning the
ability into an *asset*. They founded the Spanish Immersion Institute. The institute
llows visitors from around the country to live with a local host family and attend
lasses. Run by local youth (most of the program's tutors are teenagers, while many
tudents are adults), the goal of the four-week program is to promote cross-cultural
nderstanding. José is now studying pre-med at Yale University and hopes to
ecome a doctor.

Cirque du Soleil is an amazing circus show that pairs incredible *feats* of strength
and balance with dazzling costumes and sets. Though only in her late teens,
Kristina Ivanova has been a gymnast with Cirque du Soleil for seven years. After
six years of gymnastics training in Russia, she knew she wanted to be part of the
troupe after her father joined. When another performer left, she auditioned and
got the job. Being with the circus has *afforded* her some unusual opportunities. She
has been able to travel all over the world. And unlike many kids, Kristina is
trilingual. She speaks Russian, English, and French, the language used in Cirque
du Soleil schools.

s a rising star in the world of professional golf, **Se Ri Pak** earned the nickname
The Magic Princess." At 20, the *rookie* became one of the youngest players to
vin a major competition. Most amazingly, she accomplished this after playing the
ame for only six years. When she won, the president of South Korea sent his
ersonal congratulations. The success comes as no surprise to Se Ri, however.
he had predicted that she would win tournaments during her first year in major
ompetitions.

Read the article. Find the words in *italics* in the article.
n match each word with its meaning.

1. *liability*   a. a strength or benefit
2. *asset*   b. provide or give
3. *feat*   c. a novice or beginner
4. *afford*   d. a problem or disadvantage
5. *rookie*   e. an act that requires skill

Which of these statements are inferences (**I**)? Which are restatements (**R**)?
ich are not given (**NG**)?

1. People can learn about other cultures at the Spanish Immersion Institute.
2. José is no longer a tutor at the Spanish Immersion Institute.
3. Kristina traveled with the circus before she joined as a performer.
4. Kristina probably inherited her athletic ability from her family.
5. Se Ri Pak was 14 years old when she started playing golf.
6. Se Ri Pak lives in South Korea.

Group work Which person do you think is making the biggest contribution to society? Why?
at personal characteristics made it possible for them to achieve so much?

Challenges and accomplishments • 111

Units 15-16 Progress check

SELF-ASSESSMENT

How well can you do these things? Check (✓) the boxes.

I can	Very well	OK	A little
Give recommendations and opinions using passive modals (Ex. 1)	☐	☐	☐
Listen to, understand, and use tag questions to ask for agreement (Ex. 2)	☐	☐	☐
Identify qualities necessary to achieve certain goals (Ex. 3)	☐	☐	☐
Describe challenges with complex noun phrases containing gerunds (Ex. 3)	☐	☐	☐
Talk about your accomplishments and goals using the present perfect and future perfect (Ex. 4)	☐	☐	☐

1 DISCUSSION Setting the rules

A *Pair work* What kinds of rules do you think should be made for these places? Talk with your partner and make three rules for each. (Have fun! Don't make your rules too serious.)

a health club   an apartment building
a school   the library

B *Group work* Join another pair. Share your ideas. Do they agree?

A: People should be required to use every machine in a health club.
B: That sounds interesting. Why?
A: Well, for one thing, people would be in better shape!

2 LISTENING Social issues

A ▶ Listen to people give opinions. Check (✓) the correct responses.

1. ☐ Yes, it is.
   ☐ Yes, they are.

2. ☐ Yes, they do.
   ☐ Yes, they should.

3. ☐ Yes, we do.
   ☐ Yes, it does.

4. ☐ Yes, it does.
   ☐ Yes, it should.

5. ☐ No, they can't.
   ☐ No, it isn't.

6. ☐ No, they don't.
   ☐ No, you can't.

B *Pair work* Write tag questions for each response you did not check.

1. Stray animals are so sad, aren't they? Yes, they are.

3 DISCUSSION *What does it take?*

A *Group work* What qualities are good or bad if you want to accomplish these goals? Talk with the group and decide on two qualities for each.

Goals	Qualities		
hike around the world	adaptable	dependent	self-sufficient
conduct an orchestra	compassionate	insensitive	timid
make a movie	courageous	resourceful	unimaginative
scuba dive	cynical	rigid	upbeat

A: To hike around the world, you need to be courageous.
B: Yeah, and you can't be dependent on anyone.

B *Group work* What do you think would be the most challenging things about achieving the goals in part A? How would you overcome the challenges?

A: I think the most challenging thing about hiking around the world would be feeling lonely all the time.
B: I agree. So how would you cope with loneliness? . . .

4 ROLE PLAY *Newspaper interview*

Student A: Student B is going to interview you for the school paper. Think about your accomplishments and goals. Then answer the questions.

Student B: Imagine you are interviewing Student A for the school paper. Add two questions to the notebook. Then start the interview.

> *What have you managed to accomplish in school? What would*
>   *you like to have achieved by the time you graduate?*
> *Are you happy with your home? Do you hope you will move*
>   *someday? Where would you like to live?*
> *Have you been able to accomplish a lot in your career? Where*
>   *do you hope you'll be in five years?*
> ....
> ....

Change roles and try the role play again.

WHAT'S NEXT?

Look at your Self-assessment again. Do you need to review anything?

Interchange activities

PERSONALITY TYPES

A *Pair work* What is your personality type? Take turns using this quiz to interview each other. Then tally your answers and find out which category best describes you.

PERSONALITY QUIZ

1. **When you work on a big project, do you:**
   a. try to finish it as quickly as possible?
   b. work at it over a long period of time?
   c. put it off as long as possible?

2. **When you do something, do you:**
   a. try to do a first-class job so people will notice?
   b. do it as well as you can without worrying too much about it?
   c. do only what you must to get it done?

3. **When faced with a difficult challenge, do you:**
   a. look forward to facing it?
   b. worry about whether you can deal with it?
   c. try to avoid it?

4. **Do you think the best way to get the most out of a day is to:**
   a. do as many things as possible?
   b. take your time to get things done?
   c. do only those things you really have to?

5. **When something needs to be done, do you:**
   a. decide to do it yourself?
   b. work with others to get it done?
   c. offer to do it only if no one else will?

6. **When something doesn't work out the way you want it to, do you:**
   a. get angry with yourself and others?
   b. think calmly about what to do next?
   c. give up because it wasn't important anyway?

7. **When people take a long time to get something done, do you:**
   a. get impatient and take over?
   b. gently encourage them to get it done?
   c. let them take their time?

8. **If you compare your goals with your friends' goals, do you:**
   a. set out to do much better than they might?
   b. hope that you and they can achieve similar things in life?
   c. not care if they set higher goals for themselves than you do?

9. **When people are late for appointments, do you:**
   a. get angry and stressed out?
   b. remember that you are sometimes late, too?
   c. not worry, because you are usually late, too?

10. **When people are talking to you, do you:**
    a. not listen and think about other things?
    b. listen and enter into the conversation?
    c. let them take over and agree with everything they say?

11. **When people are expressing their ideas and opinions, do you:**
    a. step in and give your own opinions?
    b. listen and sometimes share your own ideas?
    c. listen but not add your own opinions?

SCORING Count how many A, B, and C answers your partner has. If there are . . .

more **A** answers:	This person is a superachiever.
more **B** answers:	This person is the cool and steady type.
more **C** answers:	This person is the easygoing or carefree type.

B *Group work* Compare your scores. Then suggest four basic characteristics of each personality type.

"The superachiever is the kind of person who . . .
He or she can't stand it when . . . "

A *Pair work* Imagine you and your partner are professional party planners and have been hired to organize an important dinner party. Read about each person on the guest list.

Joanie Van Buren is 42, single, and the host of the party. Wealthy and sociable, she is an art museum volunteer. She has never been married and is rarely seen without her beloved dog.

John Pradesh is 28, single, and a computer software company owner. He was recently voted "Most Promising Entrepreneur" by *Tech* magazine. He puts his career ahead of dating and marriage.

Madge Mathers is 45, married, and a gossip columnist. She's nosy, talkative, and likes to dominate the conversation. She has a good sense of humor and is Joanie's oldest friend.

Buck Eubanks is 54, a widower, and an oil tycoon. This millionaire is bossy and straightforward. His companies have been accused of destroying land to make money.

Emma Smart is 30, single, and a nuclear physicist. She's currently working on top-secret military projects. She's shy, introverted, and recently broke up with her boyfriend of four years.

Pierre is 25, single, and Joanie's favorite chef. He's friendly and ambitious, but can be very moody. He's coming to the party to get celebrities and powerful business executives to invest in his new restaurant.

Sebastiana Di Matteo is 23, single, and a world-famous movie star. She's secretly engaged to her costar in her new movie, and is often followed by photographers.

Ralph Larson is 32, married, and a "green" politician. He's egotistical, outspoken, and tends to start arguments. He's running for public office on an environmental platform.

B *Pair work* Discuss the possible seating arrangements for the party. Then complete this seating plan.

A: Let's seat Buck next to Pierre. Pierre is interested in finding investors for his new restaurant.

B: It might be better to put Buck next to Joanie. He's a widower and she's single, so . . .

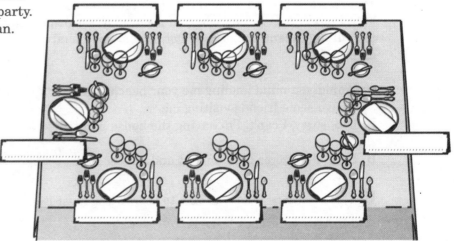

BORROWERS AND LENDERS

A Imagine you own these items. Which ones would you be willing to lend to a friend? Which ones wouldn't you lend? Check (✓) a response for each item.

mountain bike
☐ wouldn't mind lending
☐ would rather not lend

gold watch
☐ wouldn't mind lending
☐ would rather not lend

CDs
☐ wouldn't mind lending
☐ would rather not lend

sleeping bag
☐ wouldn't mind lending
☐ would rather not lend

beach house
☐ wouldn't mind lending
☐ would rather not lend

homework
☐ wouldn't mind lending
☐ would rather not lend

sports car
☐ wouldn't mind lending
☐ would rather not lend

cell phone
☐ wouldn't mind lending
☐ would rather not lend

leather jacket
☐ wouldn't mind lending
☐ would rather not lend

B *Class activity* Go around the class and take turns asking to borrow each item in part A. Say why you need it. When responding, say if you are willing to lend the item or not. If you won't lend something, give an excuse.

A: Would you mind lending me your beach house for the weekend? I have some friends visiting me.
B: Um, sorry, I can't. I'm having the house painted.
OR
B: Sure. Just come over tonight and get the key.

C *Class activity* Who was able to borrow the most items?

A DOUBLE ENDING

A Read the beginning and the two possible endings of this story.

Beginning

Ken Passell grew up in a small, working-class family in Detroit, Michigan. His father was an auto mechanic and his mother worked in a factory. When Ken was a child, he was very good with his hands.

Ending 1

The wedding was the biggest in the history of Los Angeles. After the ceremony, Ken and Cindy left on their private yacht for a honeymoon cruise to Baja, Mexico. When they return, they will live in their twenty-room mansion in Beverly Hills.

Ending 2

Ken and his wife, Cindy, were arrested in London last week. Police found more than $250,000 in cash in their suitcase. The couple insists they are innocent. "I don't know how the money got in our luggage," Ken told the police.

B *Pair work* Choose one of the endings. What do you think happened during the middle part of the story? Discuss and take notes.

C *Group work* Tell your story to another pair. Answer any follow-up questions they have.

A These statements are generally true about cultural behavior in the United States. Check (✓) those that are true in your country.

Socializing

□ 1. Women often kiss their friends on the cheek when they meet.

□ 2. It's not acceptable to ask people how much money they earn.

□ 3. People avoid asking each other about their religious beliefs.

□ 4. When invited to someone's home, people usually arrive on time or a little late.

□ 5. It's good to ask before bringing a friend or family member to a party at someone's home.

□ 6. When someone moves into a new home, it's the custom to give a "housewarming" gift.

□ 7. People usually call first before dropping by a friend's house.

□ 8. When eating in a restaurant, friends either split the cost of the meal or take turns paying.

In public

□ 9. It's OK to blow your nose quietly in public.

□ 10. It's uncommon to bargain when you buy things in stores.

At work and school

□ 11. In an office, people usually prefer to be called by their first name.

□ 12. Students remain seated when the teacher enters the classroom.

Dating and marriage

□ 13. Teenagers go out on dates.

□ 14. People decide for themselves who they will marry.

□ 15. When a couple gets married, the bride's family usually pays for the wedding and the reception.

B *Pair work* Compare your answers with a partner. For the statements you *didn't* check, why do you think these things are different in your country?

C *Group work* Can you think of an example where you (or someone you know) didn't follow the appropriate cultural behavior? What happened? Share your experiences.

A: On my last vacation, I tried to bargain for something in a store.
B: What happened?
A: I was told that the prices were fixed. It was a little embarrassing because . . .

FIXER-UPPER

Student A

A Look at this apartment. What's wrong with it? First, make
a list of as many problems as you can find in each room.

B *Pair work* Compare your lists. What are the similarities and
differences in the problems between your picture here and your
partner's picture? Ask questions to find the differences.

A: What's wrong in the living room?
B: Well, in my picture, the sofa has a hole in it. And the carpet . . .
A: Oh, really? In my picture, the sofa has a hole in it, but the carpet . . . ,
   and the wallpaper . . .

Student B

A Look at this apartment. What's wrong with it? First, make a list of as many problems as you can find in each room.

B *Pair work* Compare your lists. What are the similarities and differences in the problems between your picture here and your partner's picture? Ask questions to find the differences.

A: What's wrong in the living room?
B: Well, in my picture, the sofa has a hole in it. And the carpet . . .
A: Oh, really? In my picture, the sofa has a hole in it, but the carpet . . . , and the wallpaper . . .

MAKE YOUR VOICES HEARD!

A Read about these issues. Which one would you most likely protest?

> STARTING next month, local transit authorities will significantly raise the cost of all public transportation in and around your city.

> A POPULAR soda company has been secretly using addictive and potentially harmful chemicals in its recipe to increase sales.

> THE GOVERNMENT is negotiating the sale of portions of your country's biggest wildlife perserve to an oil-drilling company.

B *Group work* Find other students who chose the same issue. Then look at these methods of protest. Which are the most effective for the issue you chose? Complete the chart.

a demonstration

a sit-in

a petition

Method of protest	Very effective	Somewhat effective	Not effective
organize a rally or demonstration	☐	☐	☐
start an e-mail writing campaign	☐	☐	☐
stage a sit-in	☐	☐	☐
boycott a product or service	☐	☐	☐
circulate a petition	☐	☐	☐
pay for advertisements on TV or the radio	☐	☐	☐
write a letter to the editor of a newspaper	☐	☐	☐
call your local government representative	☐	☐	☐
distribute pamphlets about the issue	☐	☐	☐
hold an awareness campaign in schools	☐	☐	☐

Develop a strategy to make your voices heard using the above methods or your own ideas.

C *Class activity* How did you decide to deal with the issue? Present your group's strategy to the class.

LEARNING CURVES

A Complete this chart with information about yourself. Add one idea of your own.

two foreign languages I'd like to speak	....	....
two musical instruments I'd like to play	....	....
two dances I'd like to learn	....	....
two types of cuisine I'd like to learn how to cook	....	....
two evening courses I'd like to take	....	....
two sports I'd like to play	....	....
two skills that I'd like to improve	....	....
two	....	....

B *Class activity* Ask three classmates to help you choose between the things you wrote down in part A. Write your final choices in the chart.

Names:	....	....	....
foreign language	....	....	....
musical instrument	....	....	....
dance	....	....	....
cuisine	....	....	....
evening course	....	....	....
sport	....	....	....
skill	....	....	....
....	....	....	....

A: I don't know if I'd rather speak Portuguese or Turkish. What do you think?
B: Hmm. If I were you, I'd learn Portuguese.
A: Why Portuguese and not Turkish?
B: Well, you already know Spanish, so Portuguese might be easier to learn.

C *Class activity* Who gave the best advice? Why? Tell the class.

BECAUSE I SAID SO!

A *Pair work* Read these comments made by parents. Why do you think they feel this way? Think of two arguments to support each point of view.

> Our daughter wants to get her hair permed, but we won't let her. She's only 12!

> Our son wants to get his computer upgraded, but we don't think it's necessary. We just bought it last year!

> We won't let our daughter get her ears pierced. She has to wait until she's 18.

> Regardless of the color, we refuse to let our kids get their hair dyed.

> Our son wants to have his hair cut at an expensive salon. Why can't he just go to a regular barber?

> If our daughter insists on having her nails done, she has to pay for it herself.

A: Why do you think they won't let their daughter get her hair permed?
B: They probably think it's too expensive and that she has beautiful hair.
A: They may also feel that she . . .

B *Pair work* Now put yourselves in the children's shoes. Talk about the parents' decisions, and think of two arguments their children might make.

A: Why do you think the 12-year-old wants to get her hair permed?
B: She probably wants to keep up with her friends. It's important at that age to fit in.
A: That's true. And she might want to . . .

C *Class activity* Take a vote. Do you agree with the parents or the children? Why?

Student A

A *Pair work* Ask your partner these questions. Put a check (✓) if your partner gives the correct answer. (The correct answers are in **bold**.)

1992 Barcelona Olympics

Michelangelo's *David*

Marilyn Monroe

Test Your Knowledge

  ☐ 1. Was Julius Caesar emperor of Athens, **Rome**, or Constantinople?
  ☐ 2. What did Thomas Edison invent in 1879? Was it the television, the telephone, or the **lightbulb**?
  ☐ 3. In which year did Mexico gain its independence? Was it in 1721, **1821**, or 1921?
  ☐ 4. Where were the 1992 Olympics held? Were they in Los Angeles, **Barcelona**, or Tokyo?
  ☐ 5. When did World War I take place? Was it from 1898 to 1903, from 1911 to 1915, **or from 1914 to 1918**?
  ☐ 6. What sculptor made the famous statue of David? Was it Leonardo da Vinci, Auguste Bartholdi, or **Michelangelo**?
  ☐ 7. Who was the first human in space? Was it **Yuri Gagarin**, Alan Shepard, or John Glenn?
  ☐ 8. When were the first audio CDs put on the market? Was it in 1973, **1983**, or 1993?
  ☐ 9. What was the actress Marilyn Monroe's real name? Was it Mary Lou Dreyer, **Norma Jean Baker**, or Billy Jean Monkton?
  ☐ 10. Was Cleopatra the queen of **Egypt**, Rome, or Greece?

B *Pair work* Answer the questions your partner asks you. Then compare quizzes. Who has the most correct answers?

C *Class activity* Think of three more questions of your own. Can the rest of the class answer them?

IF THINGS WERE DIFFERENT . . .

A Choose eight people from the list. Write sentences describing things
that they have or haven't done that you wish you could change.

my father/mother   my neighbor

my brother/sister   my co-worker

my spouse   my teacher

my boyfriend/girlfriend   my boss

my best friend   my country's leader

> 1. Our teacher should have warned us before she gave us that quiz.
> 2. My boss shouldn't have made me work so late before the holiday.

B *Pair work* Share your sentences with a partner. Take turns asking
and answering questions about how things would have been different.

A: Our teacher should have warned us before she gave us that quiz.
B: Why? What would you have done if you had known about it?
A: If I'd known about it, I probably would have studied, and . . .

Student B

A *Pair work* Answer the questions your partner asks you.

B *Pair work* Ask your partner these questions. Put a check (✓) if your partner gives the correct answer. (The correct answers are in **bold**.) Then compare quizzes. Who has the most correct answers?

Laika, first dog in space

Volkswagen "Beetle"

Albert Einstein

Test Your Knowledge

- ☐ 1. When did the Wright brothers make their first airplane flight? Was it in 1893, **1903**, or 1923?
- ☐ 2. What was the first living thing in space? Was it **a dog**, a monkey, or a mouse?
- ☐ 3. When did Walt Disney make his first cartoon movie? Was it in 1920, **1938**, or 1947?
- ☐ 4. In which century did the composer Mozart live? Was it the seventeenth, **eighteenth**, or nineteenth century?
- ☐ 5. Who was the novel *Frankenstein* written by? Was it Jane Austen, John Keats, or **Mary Shelley**?
- ☐ 6. Who discovered penicillin? Was it **Alexander Fleming**, Marie Curie, or Albert Einstein?
- ☐ 7. When was the first Volkswagen "Beetle" car built? Was it during the 1920s, **the 1930s**, or the 1940s?
- ☐ 8. Who used the first magnetic compass? Was it the Portuguese, **the Chinese**, or the Dutch?
- ☐ 9. When did the British return Hong Kong to China? Was it in 1995, 1996, or **1997**?
- ☐ 10. Was the theory of relativity created by **Albert Einstein**, Charles Darwin, or Isaac Newton?

C *Class activity* Think of three more questions of your own. Can the rest of the class answer them?

ENTREPRENEURS

A *Group work* Decide on an interesting business to open with your group – for example, a video arcade, a health club, a music store, or a café.

B *Group work* What do you have to do in order to su in the business you chose? Use these questions to identify at least five different factors.

What are the most important things you need in order to run the business?
How important is the name of the business?
Do you think the location of the business is important?
How important is advertising or having a gimmick?

C *Group work* Now design a plan for the business. Determine these factors:

name	special features
product or service	slogan
location	type of advertising
decor	other considerations

A: So, what are we going to call our café?
B: I think that before we choose a name, we need to decide on a theme.
C: I agree. Almost everything else will depend on . . .

D *Class activity* Present your plan to the class. Who has the best concept?

a health club

a café

a music store

A *Pair work* Look at these pictures. What do you think might have happened in each situation? Talk about possibilities for each picture.

A: Maybe the woman thought of something funny that had happened earlier.
B: Or, she might not have understood . . .

B *Group work* Agree on one interpretation of each situation and share it with the class. Be ready to answer any questions.

A *Group work* Think about the people involved in making a movie. What does each person do?

screenwriter	composer	costume designer
director	special-effects designer	set designer
producer	stunt person	sound-effects technician
film editor	cinematographer	extra
actor	lighting technician	makeup artist

A: What does a screenwriter do?
B: That's the person that writes the script for the movie. It can be an original script or an adaptation of a book or play.

B *Group work* Imagine you are going to make a movie. What kind of movie will it be? Decide what job each person in your group will do.

A: You should be the director because you're the best leader.
B: But I'm also creative, and I'd rather be the costume designer.

C *Class activity* Present your movie idea to the class. Explain how each person will contribute to the making of the film.

a cinematographer

a costume designer

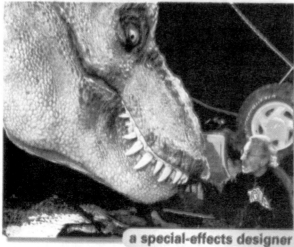

a special-effects designer

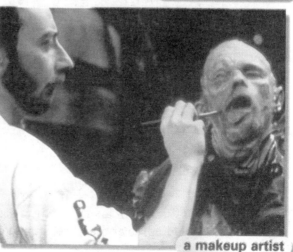

a makeup artist

A *Pair work* What punishment (if any) is appropriate for each possible offense? Complete the chart.

Offense	Punishment
1. failing to clean up after a dog	....
2. crossing the street in dangerous places	....
3. leaving trash on public streets	....
4. using a cell phone while driving	....
5. buying pirated CDs and DVDs	....
6. driving without a seat belt	....
7. riding a motorcycle without a helmet	....
8. painting graffiti on public property	....
9. stealing from your company	....
10. shoplifting	....
11. hacking into a government computer	....
12. .... (your own idea)	....

A: What do you think should be done about people who don't clean up after their dog?
B: They should be required to pay a fine.
A: I don't agree. I think . . .

possible punishments

receive a warning
spend some time in jail
pay a fine
lose a driver's license
get suspended
do community service

B *Group work* Join another pair of students. Then compare and discuss your lists. Do you agree or disagree? Try to convince each other that you are right!

A Complete this survey with information about yourself.

WHAT DO YOU THINK?

1. Do you help out in your community?
- ☐ Yes, I do regularly.
- ☐ Yes, I do from time to time.
- ☐ No, I don't right now.
- ☐ other: ....

2. Would you consider working in a developing country?
- ☐ Yes. It would be an interesting experience.
- ☐ Maybe when I'm a lot older.
- ☐ No. That's definitely not for me.
- ☐ other: ....

3. What's the best way to raise money for charities?
- ☐ through donations
- ☐ through taxes
- ☐ through special fund-raising activities
- ☐ other: ....

4. Who do you think has the greatest responsibility to support charities?
- ☐ the government
- ☐ all citizens
- ☐ the wealthy
- ☐ other: ....

5. What's the best way of improving a community?
- ☐ through education
- ☐ by creating more jobs
- ☐ by protecting the environment
- ☐ other: ....

6. Which of these things are you most concerned about?
- ☐ the environment
- ☐ crime and safety
- ☐ unemployment
- ☐ other: ....

7. Which of these activities would you prefer doing?
- ☐ helping the elderly
- ☐ helping the poor
- ☐ helping the sick
- ☐ other: ....

8. What advice would you give someone who wanted to work for a charitable organization?
- ☐ Go for it! It's one of the most rewarding things you can do.
- ☐ Be selective about who you decide to work for.
- ☐ Don't do it. It's a waste of time.
- ☐ other: ....

B *Pair work* Compare your responses. Do you and your partner have similar viewpoints?

C *Class activity* Take a class poll. Which choice was the most popular for each question? Talk about any "other" responses people added.

Units 1-16 Self-study

1 FAVORITE TEACHERS

A ▶ Lisa, Mark, and Phil are talking about teachers at their school. Listen to the conversations. Then check (✓) all the words that are true for Lisa.

> **Lisa likes teachers who are . . . .**
>
> ☐ easygoing   ☐ knowledgeable   ☐ quiet
> ☐ funny   ☐ organized   ☐ sensitive

B ▶ Listen again. What does Phil dislike about each of the teachers? Complete the sentences.

1. He can't stand it when Ms. Petty ....
2. It bothers him when Mr. Clark ....
3. He doesn't like it when Mrs. White ....

2 CAREER FAIR

A ▶ Cindy and Tim are at a career fair. What jobs are they interested in? Write **C** for Cindy, **T** for Tim, or **B** for both.

B ▶ Listen again. What do Cindy and Tim think of the jobs? Check (✓) True or False for each statement.

	True	False
1. Writing for a newspaper isn't as creative as being a TV reporter.	☐	☐
2. A TV reporter is better paid than a newspaper writer.	☐	☐
3. Working in the news isn't as rewarding as helping people.	☐	☐
4. A psychiatrist is better educated than a lawyer.	☐	☐
5. A psychiatrist has worse hours than a lawyer.	☐	☐

3 ON THE PHONE

A ▶ Listen to three telephone calls. Check (✓) the correct answers.

Who . . . ?	Ana	Jim	Liz	Alan	Zack
1. makes an invitation	☐	☐	☐	☐	☐
2. asks for a favor	☐	☐	☐	☐	☐
3. calls with an excuse	☐	☐	☐	☐	☐

B ▶ Listen again. Answer the questions.

1. What and when is the event? ....
2. What's the request? ....
3. What's the excuse? ....

4 TOGETHER AGAIN

A ▶ Listen to the news story. Check (✓) the word that best describes the situation.

☐ coincidence ☐ misfortune ☐ mystery ☐ predicament

B ▶ Listen again. Number the events from 1 to 8.

☐ Terry gave Jill a baby picture.
☐ Terry looked for her biological mother.
☐ Terry was raised by another family.
☐ Terry's father died.

☐ Jill realized that Terry was her daughter.
☐ Terry and Jill worked at the same store.
☐ Terry's mother gave her up for adoption.
☐ Terry was talking about finding her mother.

5 A TRIP ABROAD

A ▶ Listen to people talk about going to foreign countries. What is each person concerned about? Fill in the blanks.

1. _eating out in restaurants_
   a. ☐ You're expected to leave quickly if people are waiting.
   b. ☐ You're supposed to leave a tip.

2. ....
   a. ☐ You aren't supposed to arrive early.
   b. ☐ It's the custom to take off your shoes.

3. ....
   a. ☐ It's the custom to introduce your friends.
   b. ☐ You're expected to kiss people on both cheeks.

4. ....
   a. ☐ It's acceptable to approach your teacher before or after class.
   b. ☐ You aren't supposed to talk during class.

B ▶ Listen again. Check (✓) the appropriate response to each question.

6 CUSTOMER COMPLAINTS

A ▶ Listen to people talk about problems with items they bought.
What are the items? Fill in the blanks.

IMPORTANT
1. The woman's _____ hasn't been working.
It keeps going dead and the paper gets torn.
She says it needs to be fixed.

To Do...
2. The man's _____ doesn't fit well. It's
too loose around the waist. The sleeve is stained
under the arm, as well.

3. The woman's _____ keeps leaking
oil. There may be a crack somewhere. Also,
the engine keeps skipping.

4. The man's _____ isn't working very
well. The heater is too cool, and the coffee
keeps leaking out. The pot has a chip in it.

B ▶ Listen again. Correct the three mistakes in each report.

7 PROBLEM NEIGHBORHOODS

A ▶ Listen to people talk about problems in their city.
What are the problems and their causes?

Problem	Cause	Solution
1.	....	....
2.	....	....
3.	....	....

B ▶ Listen again. What solutions are proposed?

8 ONLINE CLASSES

A ▶ Susie is taking classes online this semester. Listen and
check (✓) the statements that are true.

    1. Susie is taking all of her classes online.
    2. Students don't have to do the assignments at the same time.
    3. She gets her assignments by picking them up on campus.
    4. Students can't ask the teacher questions.
    5. You take the final test online.
    6. She learns more from online classes than from regular classes.
    7. She'd rather take online classes than regular classes.

B ▶ Listen again. Correct the false statements.

9 FINDING SOLUTIONS

A ▶ Listen to the questions. What does each person need to do? Fill in the blanks.

1. *have a computer upgraded* ....
   a. ☐ It might be a good idea to upgrade your computer.
   b. ☐ One thing you could do is check out those repair shops on Sixth Avenue.

2. ....
   a. ☐ What about looking at ads for typists online?
   b. ☐ Maybe you could buy one at a printing shop.

3. ....
   a. ☐ Why don't you cut down on yoga classes?
   b. ☐ Have you thought about getting a private instructor?

4. ....
   a. ☐ What about going to a one-day tax center?
   b. ☐ Why don't you pay your taxes?

B ▶ Listen again. Check (✓) the appropriate response to each question.

10 FROM THE PAST TO THE FUTURE

A ▶ Listen to people talk about past events or happenings. Circle the type of event in column A.

A: Event/happening	B: Prediction
1. invention achievement epidemic	a. ☐ Many people will become vegetarians, because of the health risks associated with eating red meat. b. ☐ People will be eating more and more red meat, as the health benefits of beef become well known.
2. terrorist act achievement assassination	a. ☐ By 2020, people will be getting all their information from newspapers and television. The Internet will have disappeared. b. ☐ In a few years, newspapers and television will have disappeared. People will get all their information from the Internet.
3. discovery terrorist act epidemic	a. ☐ People will be using metal detectors to find precious metals. b. ☐ Soon, everyone will have to walk through a metal detector before leaving home every day.
4. invention disaster epidemic	a. ☐ Lighter, more energy-efficient cars will have replaced gas-powered cars within ten years. b. ☐ In the future, people will be driving cars that use more gas.

B ▶ Listen again. What might happen as a result of each event or happening?
Check (✓) the appropriate prediction in column B.

11 LOOKING BACK

A ▶ Listen. What did each person use to be like? Check (✓) the best word.

1. ☐ carefree   ☐ generous
2. ☐ independent   ☐ rebellious
3. ☐ immature   ☐ naive

B ▶ Listen again. Choose the sentence that each speaker might say.

1. a. ☐ If I'd been less dependent, I would have learned about money sooner.
   b. ☐ I shouldn't have gotten my first job when I was in college.
2. a. ☐ If I hadn't met Teresa, I would have gone to college.
   b. ☐ I should have treated my parents better as a teenager.
3. a. ☐ I should have traveled abroad when I was younger.
   b. ☐ If I'd traveled abroad, I wouldn't have learned about different cultures.

12 THE ART OF MAKING FRIENDS

A ▶ Listen to a psychiatrist talk about making friends.
Check (✓) the statements that are true.

☐ 1. Some people make friends easily because they know how to connect with others.
☐ 2. People who make friends easily are always clever and charming.
☐ 3. For someone to like you, you have to look good.
☐ 4. To succeed in making friends, you should show an interest in others.
☐ 5. Good friends usually look the same.

B ▶ Listen again. Correct the false statements.

13 REACTIONS

A ▶ Listen. Circle the correct answers in column A.

A	B
1. Mary should offer her teacher (**a suggestion / an excuse**).	a. ☐ Mary would have gone to class. b. ☐ Mary should have gone to class.
2. David is making (**an assumption / a prediction**) about Barbara.	a. ☐ Barbara must have been at work. b. ☐ Barbara should have been at work.
3. Bob should give Joe (**a warning / an excuse**).	a. ☐ They should have left early. b. ☐ They shouldn't have left early.
4. Katy is making (**an assumption about / a demand of**) Michael.	a. ☐ Michael should have told him. b. ☐ Michael must have told him.

B ▶ Listen again. Check (✓) the most logical sentence in column B.

14 AN ANIMATED FILM

A ▶ Listen to the interview. Answer the questions.

1. What does Jim do?
2. What does the director of animated films do?
3. What does an animator do?

B ▶ Listen again. Number the steps from 1 to 8.

☐ A director is hired.　　　　　　☐ The script is written.
☐ A storyboard is made.　　　　　☐ Actors record the characters' voices.
☐ The scenes are put together.　　☐ The cels are photographed on the backgrounds.
☐ The backgrounds are created.　　☐ The pictures of the characters are drawn.

15 WHAT DO YOU THINK?

A ▶ Listen to people talk about social issues and problems. What is each person concerned about? Fill in the blanks.

1. ....
   a. ☐ I agree. People must be allowed to quit school in seventh grade.
   b. ☐ I agree. Laws must be passed to make people stay in school.

2. ....
   a. ☐ Yes, it is. Once I had to wait for over an hour, too.
   b. ☐ Yes, they should. There's no reason why they can't be on time.

3. ....
   a. ☐ Yes, they are. Dance clubs should be allowed to stay open late.
   b. ☐ Yes, they are. Dance clubs shouldn't be allowed to stay open late.

4. ....
   a. ☐ No, I don't. People ought not to be required, only encouraged.
   b. ☐ No, I don't. I think people should be required to vote.

B ▶ Listen again. Check (✓) the appropriate response.

16 CHALLENGES

A ▶ Listen to Paulo talk about the Peace Corps. What are his accomplishments? What are his goals? Write **A** or **G**.

.... 1. be accepted by the community
.... 2. learn about another culture
.... 3. live in a different country
.... 4. speak the languages

B ▶ Listen again. Correct the statements.

1. One of the most challenging things about living abroad is finding time to write to your friends and family.
2. One of the easiest things is learning the local languages.
3. The greatest reward of working with these people is learning things that I couldn't learn on my own.

Self-study audio scripts

1 Favorite teachers

A Lisa, Mark, and Phil are talking about teachers at their school. Listen to the conversations. Then check all the words that are true for Lisa.

PHIL: Hi, Mark. Did you get your class schedule?
MARK: Hi, Phil. Hi, Lisa. Yeah, I just picked it up.
LISA: So, who do you have?
MARK: Let me see. I have Ms. Petty for history.
LISA: Oh, Ms. Petty is really smart. I like teachers who know a lot of different things.
MARK: You had her, too, Phil. What do you think?
PHIL: She's good. But I can't stand it when she assigns a ton of homework on Fridays . . . just in time for the weekend! Who else do you have?
MARK: Um, I have Mr. Clark for English.
PHIL: He's great. You just can't hear him! It bothers me when he speaks too softly.
LISA: He does speak quietly. But I like him. He's the kind of teacher you can talk to really easily.
MARK: And I have Mrs. White for algebra.
LISA: Oh, she's hilarious! I love teachers who have a good sense of humor. She makes algebra fun.
PHIL: Yeah. I like her, too. But I don't like it when she forgets my name.
LISA: Oh, Phil. That happened *once*.

B Listen again. What does Phil dislike about each of the teachers? Complete the sentences.

2 Career fair

A Cindy and Tim are at a career fair. What jobs are they interested in? Write **C** for Cindy, **T** for Tim, or **B** for both.

CINDY: There are so many jobs! Working in the news could be fun. I'd love being a TV reporter.
TIM: Are you kidding? Being a TV reporter seems kind of boring. I don't like television news.
CINDY: So what would *you* like to do in the news?
TIM: I think I'd enjoy writing for a newspaper. It's more creative than being a TV reporter.
CINDY: Yes, but a TV reporter earns more.
TIM: What about being a lawyer? I think helping people is more rewarding than working in the news.
CINDY: A lawyer? Why?
TIM: Well, I think lawyers can really help people. And I like studying and being in school.
CINDY: Hmm. I like helping people, but I think I'd rather be a psychiatrist or something.
TIM: A psychiatrist. I think I'd like that, too. And psychiatrists go to school as much as lawyers.
CINDY: And psychiatrists don't work as late.

B Listen again. What do Cindy and Tim think of the jobs? Check True or False for each statement.

3 On the phone

A Listen to three telephone calls. Check the correct answers.

1. LIZ: Hello.
   JIM: Hi, Liz. It's Jim.
   LIZ: Hi, Jim. What's up?
   JIM: Well, I have tickets for a play tonight. It's called *A Cold Night*. Are you interested?
   LIZ: Oh, I've heard about *A Cold Night*. Sure.
   JIM: Great. Meet me at the Douglas Theater at 7:30. The show is at 8:00.
   LIZ: OK! See you then.

2. LIZ: Hello.
   ALAN: Liz? This is Alan.
   LIZ: Alan, I can barely hear you. Where are you?
   ALAN: I'm at a gas station. My car broke down, and I can't get a tow truck. Could you pick me up?
   LIZ: Oh, I'm supposed to meet Jim in an hour.
   ALAN: It won't take long, I promise.
   LIZ: Oh, OK. Just tell me where you are. . . .

3. ZACK: Hello.
   ANA: Hi, Zack, it's Ana. Is Jim there?
   ZACK: I'm sorry. You just missed him.
   ANA: Uh-oh. Liz has been trying to call.
   ZACK: Oh, I was online.
   ANA: I'm calling because her cell phone died. She can't meet Jim at the theater because she got stuck in traffic. Could you tell Jim she's sorry?
   ZACK: Sure thing.

B Listen again. Answer the questions.

4 Together again

A Listen to the news story. Check the word that best describes the situation.

MAN: Tonight, the story of a mother and daughter who were reunited after 20 years. Terry Harris never knew her biological parents. Her father died suddenly, and her mother gave her up for adoption when she was only a year old. Terry was raised by a loving family, but she always wondered what happened to her "real" mother. As a teenager, Terry had searched for her mother, but wasn't able to find her.

Jill Johnson, Terry's biological mother, had also spent many years looking for her daughter, with no success. But now, the two women live one-half mile from each other. And even though they had been working together at a local store for more than a year, they didn't realize they were mother and daughter.

One day at work, Terry was telling Jill about the search for her mother. Jill told her she knew someone who could help. Terry gave Jill a picture of herself as a baby. When Jill took it home and compared it with photos of her daughter, she realized that Terry was her child. The next day, Jill told Terry the news, and they were joyfully reunited.

B Listen again. Number the events from 1 to 8.

5 A trip abroad

A Listen to people talk about going to foreign countries. What is each person concerned about? Fill in the blanks.

1. MAN: Something I'm worried about is eating out in restaurants. In my country, after we've finished eating, we often stay at the table and talk for hours. In the United States, do you have to leave the table after your meal?

2. WOMAN: I'm going to be studying in Japan next year. One thing I'm nervous about is visiting my hosts' home for the first time. When I arrive at their house, what should I do?

3. MAN: My fiancée and I are traveling to Paris next year. I'm going to meet her parents. One thing I'm insecure about is meeting people for the first time. I'm afraid I'll do the wrong thing. What do you do in France when you're introduced to people?

4. WOMAN: I'm going to college in the United States next year. One thing that I'm worried about is behaving correctly in school. I wonder if it's OK to talk to the teacher after class.

B Listen again. Check the appropriate response to each question.

6 Customer complaints

A Listen to people talk about problems with items they bought. What are the items? Fill in the blanks.

1. WOMAN: I bought a new fax machine and it isn't working right. It keeps breaking down and the paper gets jammed. It needs to be replaced.

2. MAN: I bought a wool sweater from a fancy store. I thought it fit well, but the first time I wore it I noticed it was too tight around the chest. Then I noticed that the sleeve was torn under the arm.

3. WOMAN: This truck keeps leaking water. I think there may be a hole somewhere. And the engine needs to be adjusted. It keeps overheating.

4. MAN: I just bought this coffeemaker. It's a very expensive one, too, but it's not working very well. The heater is too hot, and the coffee keeps burning. The pot has a small crack in it, too.

B Listen again. Correct the three mistakes in each report.

7 Problem neighborhoods

A Listen to people talk about problems in their city. What are the problems and their causes?

1. MAN: The neighborhood I live in used to be so pretty. But now many of the houses on my street are being deserted due to increasing crime. It's depressing to walk down the street. It seems like such a waste when so many people need homes. I think one thing to do is to give the homes to organizations that fix them up. You know, the kind of organizations that turn them into public housing.

2. WOMAN: I get so angry. Some animals in the neighborhood are being mistreated by their owners. One dog is tied up all day with no water! I think the best way to make owners take responsibility is to report them to the police. Then they'll know they're being watched!

3. MAN: The beautiful old school in our neighborhood has been closed for the past five years. It's a historic building, and now it's being destroyed as a result of vandalism. One thing to do with it is turn it into a community center. That way, neighborhood families will have a place to go and have fun.

B Listen again. What solutions are proposed?

8 Online classes

A Susie is taking classes online this semester. Listen and check the statements that are true.

MAN: Hey, Susie, how are your classes this year?
SUSIE: Great! And I'm taking some of them online. It's a different way of studying, and I'm really enjoying it.
MAN: Really? How are online classes different from regular classes?
SUSIE: Well, for one thing, there's no class time, so you choose when you want to do the assignments.
MAN: Huh. How does that work?
SUSIE: It's pretty cool. You get your assignments by downloading them off the Web. And you turn in your work by posting it online. Students can ask the teacher questions over e-mail.
MAN: And are there any tests?
SUSIE: Yes, there's a final test. You have to take that in a classroom.
MAN: Do you think you learn as much from an online class as you do from a regular class?
SUSIE: Sure. Actually, I think I might learn more, because I spend more time studying.
MAN: So overall, do you prefer to take online classes or regular classes?
SUSIE: Oh, I like to take both. With online classes, you learn perseverance by studying independently. On the other hand, with regular classes, you practice communication because you're working with other people.
MAN: Well, it sounds like an interesting experience.
SUSIE: Yes, it is.

B Listen again. Correct the false statements.

9 Finding solutions

A Listen to the questions. What does each person need to do? Fill in the blanks.

1. MAN: My computer is so slow, and I can't put up with it any longer! It takes forever just to download one Web page. Do you know where I can have it upgraded?

2. WOMAN: I'm so busy! I haven't finished writing my essay for history class, and it's due tomorrow! I can finish it in time, but I'll never have time to type it. Do you know where I can have it typed?

3. MAN: I can't keep up with the other people in my yoga class. All the students seem like they know what they're doing, but I'm always behind. What should I do?

4. WOMAN: City taxes are due in a week, and I'm really busy at work. I don't have any time to take care of my finances right now. Where can I get my taxes done quickly?

B Listen again. Check the appropriate response to each question.

10 From the past to the future

A Listen to people talk about past events or happenings. Circle the type of event in column A.

1. MAN: Mad cow disease was first discovered in British cows in 1986. During the 1990s, the disease spread very quickly. It was discovered that humans can contract a form of the disease by eating meat from infected cows. By 2004, there were more than 150 confirmed cases of this disease in people.

2. WOMAN: The Internet is an amazing global tool. Since the early 1990s, vast technological advances have made it possible for people from all over the world to share news, information, culture, and entertainment in a matter of seconds.

3. MAN: Increased bombings and explosions around the world have been responsible for the deaths of many innocent people. The threat of attack by members of rebel groups is a major topic of discussion among world leaders.

4. WOMAN: Recent technology has made it possible for cars that use alternative energy sources to compete with regular, gas-powered cars. Lighter, alternative-energy cars use less harmful sources of energy and are attractive to people who want to conserve the earth's resources. These cars have become faster – and usable for longer periods of time.

B Listen again. What might happen as a result of each event or happening? Check the appropriate prediction in column B.

11 Looking back

A Listen. What did each person use to be like? Check the best word.

1. MAN: Before I got my first job, my parents paid for everything. I never thought about money. So until I started working, I hadn't realized how much things really cost. Now I worry about money a lot. Even at the supermarket, I'm careful about the choices I make. For example, I would love to eat only organic vegetables. But in many cases, they're very expensive. I try to stick to my budget!

2. MAN: I used to skip classes and fight with my parents all the time. They were so worried about me. But the moment I met Teresa, I started to grow up. She was much more mature than I was at the time, and she was a very good influence on me. I started studying and got into college. Now I even get along with my parents!

3. WOMAN: I used to assume that people in other countries thought and behaved the same way as I did. Once I traveled abroad, I realized how little I knew about other cultures. I learned to respect other people's way of doing things, and I learned a lot about myself in the process.

B Listen again. Choose the sentence that each speaker might say.

12 The art of making friends

A Listen to a psychiatrist talk about making friends. Check the statements that are true.

MAN: For some people, making friends is easy. For others, it can be a struggle. It's easy for people who know how to connect with others. But you don't need to be clever or charming to make friends. People who make friends easily know how to be themselves. There's an old saying: "A friend is someone who knows you well – and likes you anyway."

There are three simple things you can do to make friends. First, you have to like yourself. Make a list of your strengths, talents, and accomplishments. That way, when you meet new people, you'll know what you have to share.

Next, learn how to listen. For friendships to succeed, you need to show an interest in others. Ask questions about other people.

Finally, it's a good idea to join a club or take a class. That way, you meet people who have similar interests. Good friends usually like the same things.

B Listen again. Correct the false statements.

13 Reactions

A Listen. Circle the correct answers in column A.

1. MARY: I feel so guilty.
   MAN: What's wrong?
   MARY: Oh, I missed class today. I just didn't feel like going.

2. DAVID: Have you seen Barbara recently?
   WOMAN: No. She's been working a lot lately.
   DAVID: I tried to call her yesterday, but she didn't answer. I bet she'll call me back tomorrow.

3. BOB: We're really busy today – 12 deliveries.
   WOMAN: So what time do we have to leave?
   BOB: Well, we should have left an hour ago, but Joe's not here yet. He's late again.

4. KATY: I'm sorry you didn't make it to the party.
   MAN: What party? I didn't know about a party.
   KATY: Oh! Michael must have forgotten to tell you.

B Listen again. Check the most logical sentence in column B.

14 An animated film

A Listen to the interview. Answer the questions.

INTERVIEWER: Welcome to *Job Talk*. We're talking to Jim Harris, who works on animated films. Thanks for joining us, Jim. So what do you do, exactly?
JIM: I'm a film editor. I'm the person who puts the animated movie together.
INTERVIEWER: How is an animated film different from a regular movie?
JIM: Well, actually, they're very similar.
INTERVIEWER: Take us through the process.
JIM: Well, first, just like in a regular film, a script is written. You have to start with a good script.
INTERVIEWER: Of course, and it has to be funny.
JIM: Exactly. Then a director is hired.
INTERVIEWER: Now, what *does* the director of animated films do? Direct the drawings?
JIM: Ha! No, the director, who is probably the most important person, manages the process. He helps develop the characters and works with the actors.
INTERVIEWER: So what happens next?
JIM: Well, drawings are made to illustrate the story, to show what happens. This is called a storyboard. It's sort of like a rehearsal. When that's done, the animation can begin. I'll tell you how we do it the old-fashioned way. It's more interesting.
INTERVIEWER: Oh yeah? Why?
JIM: Well, it's all computerized now. So first, in the old way, actors record the characters' voices in a recording studio. The whole script is recorded.
INTERVIEWER: Then what?
JIM: Then, the backgrounds are created. It's like building the sets for a play.
INTERVIEWER: Sounds fun. What's next?
JIM: Well, the animation begins. First, pictures of the characters are drawn. The animator draws the pictures on a clear plastic called *celluloid*. That's why they're called cels. Each picture is drawn on a separate cel.
INTERVIEWER: Huh. Then what?
JIM: OK. Here's where it gets fun. They put each cel on top of a background picture and take a photograph. They do this many times. When all the photographs are put together, it looks like the characters are moving.

INTERVIEWER: That's so exciting! So that's that?
JIM: Not quite. The director and I have to put the scenes together so that they match the sound. The voices have to match the characters' movements. Once the sound has been added to the film, *that's* that!
INTERVIEWER: Fascinating. Thanks for talking to us.

B Listen again. Number the steps from 1 to 8.

15 What do you think?

A Listen to people talk about social issues and problems. What is each person concerned about? Fill in the blanks.

1. MAN: In my country, people are allowed to quit school in the seventh grade. The illiteracy rate is enormous. I think people should be required to finish school. Everyone ought to be able to read.

2. WOMAN: Sometimes I have to wait over an hour for a bus. They should improve the public transportation in this city. It's ridiculous, isn't it?

3. MAN: I get off work around 11:00 at night. Last Friday, I wanted to go dancing. But because of the new noise pollution laws, the clubs have to close at midnight. Those laws are stupid, aren't they?

4. WOMAN: In the United States, you're allowed to vote when you turn 18, but many people don't. I think people should be required to participate in elections. Don't you?

B Listen again. Check the appropriate response.

16 Challenges

A Listen to Paulo talk about the Peace Corps. What are his accomplishments? What are his goals? Write **A** or **G**.

WOMAN: So, Paulo, you've been in the Peace Corps two months now, right? Why did you join?
PAULO: I wanted to help people, and learn about another culture firsthand.
WOMAN: And have you accomplished that?
PAULO: Well, I haven't been here long enough to really learn about the people. I hope I'll have learned more about them by the end of the year.
WOMAN: Has it been hard?
PAULO: Well, one of the most challenging things about living abroad is being far away from your friends and family. I write to them almost every day. Oh! You know what's one of the most difficult things? Speaking the local languages.
WOMAN: Why is that?
PAULO: I thought I would need to learn just one, but each village has a different dialect or language.
WOMAN: Oh, wow. That's got to be difficult.
PAULO: But I'm starting to learn. Some of my new friends are helping me. I feel I've managed to be accepted by the community already.
WOMAN: Good for you, that's great.
PAULO: Thanks! And the greatest reward of working with these people is helping them learn things that they couldn't learn on their own.

B Listen again. Correct the statements.

Self-study answer key

1

A easygoing, funny, knowledgeable

B 1. assigns too much homework on Fridays
2. speaks too softly
3. forgets his name

2

A 1. T 2. T 3. B 4. C

B 1. F 2. T 3. T 4. F 5. F

3

A

	Ana	Jim	Liz	Alan	Zack
makes an invitation		✓			
asks for a favor				✓	
calls with an excuse	✓				

B 1. The event is a play, tonight at 8.
2. Alan asks Liz to pick him up.
3. Ana calls to tell Jim that Liz is stuck in traffic.

4

A coincidence

B 7 Terry gave Jill a baby picture.
4 Terry looked for her biological mother.
3 Terry was raised by another family.
1 Terry's father died.
8 Jill realized that Terry was her daughter.
5 Terry and Jill worked at the same store.
2 Terry's mother gave her up for adoption.
6 Terry was talking about finding her mother.

5

A/B 1. eating out in restaurants / a
2. arriving at someone's home for the first time / b
3. meeting people for the first time / b
4. behaving correctly in school / a

6

A/B
1. <u>fax machine</u>
~~going dead~~	breaking down
~~torn~~	jammed
~~fixed~~	replaced

2. <u>wool sweater</u>
~~loose~~	tight
~~waist~~	chest
~~stained~~	torn

3. <u>truck</u>
~~oil~~	water
~~crack~~	hole
~~skipping~~	overheating

4. <u>coffeemaker</u>
~~cool~~	hot
~~leaking out~~	burning
~~chip~~	crack

7

A/B

Problem	Cause	Solution
1. houses are being deserted	increasing crime	turn homes into public housing
2. animals are being mistreated	irresponsible owners	report owners to the police
3. school is being destroyed	vandalism	turn into a community center

8

A Numbers 2 and 6 are true.

B 1. ~~all~~ some
3. ~~picking them up on campus~~ downloading them off the Web
4. ~~can't ask the teacher questions~~ can ask the teacher questions over e-mail
5. ~~online~~ in a classroom
7. ~~online classes than regular classes~~ both

9

A/B 1. have his computer upgraded / b
2. have her essay typed / a
3. keep up in yoga class / b
4. have her taxes done / a

10

A/B 1. epidemic / a   3. terrorist act / b
2. achievement / b   4. invention / a

11

A 1. carefree 2. rebellious 3. naive

B 1. a 2. b 3. a

12

A Numbers 1 and 4 are true.

B 2. ~~are always clever and charming~~ know how to be themselves
3. ~~look good~~ like yourself
5. ~~look the same~~ like the same things

13

A/B 1. an excuse / b   3. a warning / a
2. a prediction / a   4. an assumption about / a

14

A 1. He's a film editor (he puts the film together).
2. The director manages the process of making the film (develops characters and works with actors).
3. The animator draws pictures of the characters.

B 2 A director is hired.
3 A storyboard is made.
8 The scenes and sound are put together.
5 The backgrounds are created.
1 The script is written.
4 Actors record the characters' voices.
7 The cels are photographed on the backgrounds.
6 The pictures of the characters are drawn.

15

A/B 1. illiteracy / b   3. noise pollution laws / a
2. public transportation / a   4. voting (or elections) / a

16

A 1. A 2. G 3. A 4. G

B 1. ~~finding time to write to~~ being far away from
2. ~~easiest~~ most difficult
3. ~~learning things I couldn't learn on my own~~ helping them learn things they couldn't learn on their own

Appendix

Irregular verbs

Present	Past	Past Participle	Present	Past	Past Participle
(be) am/is, are	was, were	been	leave	left	left
become	became	become	lend	lent	lent
begin	began	begun	let	let	let
bite	bit	bitten	light	lit	lit
blow	blew	blown	lose	lost	lost
break	broke	broken	make	made	made
bring	brought	brought	meet	met	met
build	built	built	pay	paid	paid
burn	burned	burned	put	put	put
buy	bought	bought	quit	quit	quit
catch	caught	caught	read	read	read
choose	chose	chosen	run	ran	run
come	came	come	say	said	said
cost	cost	cost	see	saw	seen
cut	cut	cut	sell	sold	sold
do	did	done	send	sent	sent
dream	dreamed/dreamt	dreamed/dreamt	shine	shined/shone	shined/shone
drink	drank	drunk	shoot	shot	shot
drive	drove	driven	show	showed	shown
eat	ate	eaten	sink	sank	sunk
fall	fell	fallen	sit	sat	sat
feel	felt	felt	speak	spoke	spoken
fight	fought	fought	spend	spent	spent
find	found	found	stand	stood	stood
fly	flew	flown	steal	stole	stolen
forget	forgot	forgotten	stick	stuck	stuck
forgive	forgave	forgiven	sweep	swept	swept
get	got	gotten	swim	swam	swum
give	gave	given	take	took	taken
go	went	gone	teach	taught	taught
grow	grew	grown	tear	tore	torn
have	had	had	tell	told	told
hear	heard	heard	think	thought	thought
hold	held	held	throw	threw	thrown
hurt	hurt	hurt	upset	upset	upset
keep	kept	kept	wake	woke	woken
know	knew	known	wear	wore	worn
lay	laid	laid	write	wrote	written

Acknowledgments

Illustrations

Jessica Abel IA6
Rob De Bank 6, 16 (*bottom*), 60, 61
Tim Foley 58, 76, 88 (*top*), SS11
Travis Foster 14, 18, 90, 95, 105, IA4, SS9
Jeff Grunewald 37 (*jeans*)
Adam Hurwitz 16 (*top*), 19
Randy Jones *v*, 10, 11, 25, 27, 32, 33, 40, 44 (*top*), 52, 53, 64, 68, 79, 80, 83, 84, 86, 88 (*bottom*), 89, 94, 102, 103, 109, 112, IA8, IA13, IA15

Mark Kaufman 37 (*all except jeans*), 87
Jeff Moores 59, 75, SS3
Scott Pollack IA9
Dan Vasconcellos 28, 29, 36, 43, 44 (*bottom*), 67, 91, 96, 99, 101
William Waitzman IA11
Sam Whitehead 20, 21, 38, 39, 72, 86, IA2
Jeff Wong 2, 5, 26, 30, 47

Photo credits

4 (*top*) © Digital Vision; (*bottom*) © Brian Bailey/Getty Images
7 © Brian Baily/Getty Images
9 (*top to bottom*) © Novastock/Index Stock; © Jeff Greenberg/Age Fotostock; © David Langley/Corbis; © Cristobal Herrera/AP/Wide World Photos
12 (*left to right*) © MTPA Stock/Masterfile; © Greg Pease/Getty Images; © Vic Bider/PhotoEdit
13 © Getty Images
15 (*left*) © Michael Newman/PhotoEdit; (*right*) © Punchstock
17 © Jett Britnell/Getty Images
19 © Romilly Lockyer/Getty Images
23 © Jeff Hunter/Getty Images
30 © Lifestock/Getty Images
31 © Kraig Lieb/Lonely Planet
34 (*left*) © Frann Jazombek/Envision; (*right*) © R. Cord/H. Armstrong Roberts
35 © Michael Prince/Getty Images
41 (*all photos*) Courtesy of KATU/Oregon
42 © Parrot Pascal/Corbis Sygma
45 (*top row, left to right*) © Val Corbett/Getty Images; © Gary Buss/Getty Images; © Don Spiro/Getty Images; (*bottom row, left*) © Baumgartner Olivia/Corbis Sygma; (*bottom row, middle and right*) © Telegraph Color Library/Getty Images
46 © Susan Steinkamp/Corbis
48 (*top row, left to right*) © Bob Daemmrich/The Image Works; © Peter Cade/Getty Images; (*bottom right*) © Joel Stettenheim/Corbis © Paul Thomas/Getty Images
49 © Anna Zuckerman/Envision
51 (*top*) © Michal Heron/Corbis; (*bottom*) © Katsumi Kasahara/AP/Wide World Photos
54 (*top*) © Jeffry W. Myers/Corbis; (*bottom*) © Alan Becker/Getty Images
55 © Comstock
57 © Shotgun/Corbis
62 (*left to right*) © Tom Raymond/Getty Images; © Steve Chenn/Corbis; © David Ash/Getty Images
64 (*left to right*) © Bettman/Corbis; © AP/Wide World Photos; © Dennis Hallinan/Alamy; © Time Life Pictures/Getty Images; © Topham/The Image Works; © George Kerrigan/Digital Eyes
65 (*top*) © SuperStock; (*bottom*) © NASA/JPL/AP/Wide World Photos
66 © AFP/Getty Images
69 © Ed Honowitz/Getty Images
70 © Getty Images
71 (*top*) © Paul A. Souders/Corbis; (*bottom*) © Punchstock

73 © Juan Silva/Getty Images
74 © Chuck Savage/Corbis
77 (*left to right*) © Steve Prezant/Corbis; © SuperStock; © Emmanuel Faure/SuperStock
80 © Gruber/FWD/Retna
81 © Scott Gries/Getty Images
85 © Kelly/Mooney Photography/Corbis
92 © H.J. Morrill/Index Stock Imagery
93 (*top*) © Jon Feingersh/Masterfile; (*bottom*) © David H. Wells/Corbis
94 © Jenna Issacson/Columbia Daily Tribune/AP/Wide World Photos
97 © Sherwin Crasto/Reuters
99 (*left*) © Getty Images; (*right*) © Shuji Kobayashi/Getty Images
102 © Chip Henderson/Getty Images
104 © Ian Shaw/Getty Images
106 (*left to right*) © Santosh Basak/Getty Images; © Victoria Brynner/Getty Images; © Dave Chancellor/Alpha/Globe Photos
108 © Getty Images
109 © Stuart Cohen/The Image Works
110 (*left to right*) © Jerry Amster/SuperStock; © Nancy Santullo/Corbis; © James McLoughlin/Getty Images
111 (*left*) © Cirque du Soleil Inc.; (*right, top*) courtesy of the Spanish Immersion Institute; (*right, bottom*) © Kim Kyung-Hoon/Reuters/Corbis
113 © Kevin T. Gilbert/Corbis
IA3 (*top row, left to right*) © Getty Images; © Duncan Walker/Istock; © Chaleerat Ngamchalee/Istock; (*middle row, left to right*) © Lego/Getty Images; © Jan Butchofsky-Houser/Corbis; (*bottom row, left to right*) © Romilly Lockyer/Getty Images; © George Kerrigan/Digital Eyes; © White Packert/Getty Images
IA5 (*left to right*) © Yellow Dog Productions/Getty Images; © Getty Images; © Nancy Ney/Corbis
IA7 (*left to right*) © Nicole Rosenthal/AP/Wide World Photos; © Mike Fiala/AP/Wide World Photos; © Christian Keenan/Getty Images
IA10A (*left to right*) © Robert E. Daemmrich/Getty Images; © Galleria dell' Academia, Florence/SuperStock; © Getty Images
IA10B (*left to right*) © NASA/AP/Wide World Photos; © Hulton Archive/Getty Images; © SuperStock
IA12 (*top*) © Creatas; (*bottom left*) © Paul Thomas/Getty Images; (*bottom right*) © Corbis
IA14 (*clockwise from top left*) © HBO/Getty Images; © Kelly/Mooney Photography/Corbis; © Orion Pictures/courtesy of Everett Collection; © MCA/Universal Pictures/courtesy of Everett Collection
SS2 (*all photos*) © Punchstock
SS14 © Douglas Kirkland/Corbis
SS16 © Lars Howlett/Aurora